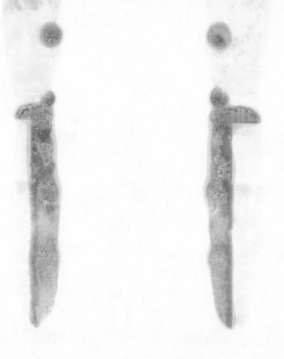

MAN'S

VICTORIOUS SPIRIT

It is with great appreciation that I acknowledge that this manuscript became possible through the understanding and affection of many people, and especially three -- my Mother, Rowena and Tom.

MAN'S
VICTORIOUS SPIRIT

How to Release the Victory Within You

by

JACK H. HOLLAND, Ph.D.

Monterey, California
Hudson-Cohan Publishing Company
1971

Copyright 1971
Hudson-Cohan Publishing Company
First Federal Court Adobe
Monterey, California

First printing   September, 1971
Second printing   October, 1971
Third printing   June, 1972

ISBN: 0-87852-001-5
Library of Congress Catalog Number: 76-179668

CHURCH OF RELIGIOUS SCIENCE
907 KNOB HILL AVENUE
REDONDO BEACH, CA 90277

TABLE OF CONTENTS

PART ONE - THE QUESTION

How to Release the Victory Within You

PART TWO - THE ANSWER

Aspects and Manifestation of *Releasing Man's Victorious Spirit:*

"'Things beyond our seeing, things beyond our hearing, things beyond our imaginings, all prepared by God for those who love him', these it is that God has revealed to us through the Spirit."

-I Corinthians 2:9,10

"...every child of God is victor over the godless world. The victory that defeats the world is our faith, for who is victor over the world but he who believes...?"

-I John 5:4,5

INTRODUCTION

On all sides today one hears the most negative of expressions concerning man, man's relationship with others and man's future. Everywhere one turns there seems to be despair regardless of whether one is talking to the most affluent in society, the most economically impoverished, youth, the elderly, etc. The problems of society - no matter where in the world one searches - seem to be unsolvable. There is the world-wide drug problem, the world-wide economic strain, the world-wide ecological crisis coupled with a population crisis; there are wars and threats of war. Everywhere one seems to find despair and negatives concerning finding a solution or solutions to problems. Probably nowhere is this "negativity" more apparent than among the expressed followers of organized religion whether one is speaking of the followers of the Eastern religions or the followers of the Judaic-Christian religions of the West. The expression, "God is dead", is not unique to the Western World.

Yet, amongst this great despair, this great "negativity", one sees "sparks" of harmony, "sparks" of human understanding, "sparks" of joy and real happiness. In virtually every case where one finds this element of joy it has stemmed from some effective inter-personal communication and from an awareness that there is a Spirit within all men that is truly victorious - victorious over all adversity, all trial and all tribulation. This Spirit can be tapped by all men but unfortunately has been tapped by few. However, when one studies the histories of truly happy men, of men who have truly accomplished something meaningful in life and for life, one immediately becomes aware that these men have learned to "tap" the victorious and triumphant Spirit that lies dormant in the more common man. These men have found a very literal meaning in Paul's admonition in II Corinthians 4:4, "Their unbelieving minds are so blinded by the god of this passing age, that the gospel of the glory of Christ, who is the very image of God, cannot dawn upon them and bring them light."

I choose to believe that Paul was warning us today as much as he was the people of more than nineteen hundred years ago. Certainly, most of us are blinded by the materialism of today and we despair. Most of us are constantly looking for "crutches" outside ourselves. We are looking for simplistic answers which are not to be found among the "gods" of this passing age - money, drugs, education without understanding, all-knowing science, sensual excesses, etc. Certainly the Western World is not unique in seeking "crutches" nor is Christianity the only religion that has warned men of the dangers of looking only to its current "gods" for basic answers to finding peace, harmony and joy. All have taught that man has within him a victorious Spirit which can rise above any adversity and can bring peace, harmony, joy, enthusiasm and a sense of oneness with all other men. The manner recommended for arriving at this "victory" varies with the culture and the specific leader who founded the religion *but* all agree that it is there ready for our salvation. The word, salvation, explains a great deal concerning Paul's statement. Webster's Dictionary gives as a meaning of "salvation" the following: "liberation from clinging to the phenomenal world of appearance and final union with ultimate reality." What man is truly seeking in his constant quest for answers to all problems - even those that seem the most insurmountable - is a final union with ultimate reality, with Spirit. In that final union, of course, man becomes triumphant and is truly victorious. Then man can really begin to solve the problems that seem so insurmountable today, and man can find a meaning in, and for, life.

Many may well feel while reading this book that "seeking Spirit" is not a logical or a realistic manner in which to search for solutions to today's problems. I hope to awaken an interest in this method of finding answers in all who will remain with me through these various discourses. Certainly the way the world has tried to solve problems through materialism and "education" has been fruitless. Man has come far in terms of solving his creature comfort problems, in making his physical life easier, in expanding his knowledge of the material world and material things; but man has made little or no progress in developing his spiritual awareness (or the "oversoul" of Emerson or the "collective consciousness" of Jung). It is my belief that it is only when man has learned to develop equally his three "sides" - mind, body, and spirit - that he will find peace, harmony, joy and the answers to the tremendous problems that face him on the material level. In the past one hundred years man has made giant strides in regard to developing the mind (information collecting) through mass education - strides that were beyond the fondest dreams of learned men as late as the year 1900. In the past one hundred years understanding and knowledge of the human body and how to treat it has revolutionized all previous awareness of medicine, nutrition, genetics, biology and bio-chemistry. However, we still do not treat our bodies as we know they should be treated as is witnessed by the mass malnutrition among even our most affluent. Nevertheless, man has made giant leaps forward in regard to understanding his body. In the "trinity" of body, mind and spirit the only element with which man has not made progress - indeed, he has probably retrogressed - is Spirit. It is Spirit which man must learn to release, it is here that answers lie, it is here where creativity awaits, it is here where peace, harmony and joy are to be found. Once one recognizes that the Spirit will be victorious and triumphant then all three elements of the trinity take their proper places and truly life becomes one of meaning and purpose.

PART ONE

"THE QUESTION"

CHAPTER ONE

The Senseless Sixties and the Search
for Meaning in Life

There is every possibility that the Nineteen Sixties will become known to future generations as the "senseless Sixties" which will go right along with the "gay Nineties", the "terrible Thirties" and the "roaring Twenties" as part of man's "lexicon of eras." In so many respects man seemed to have lost perspective, common sense and any degree of "selflessness" during the decade of the Sixties. It matters not whether one looks at the United States or at any other part of the world, the "senseless" aspects of the Sixties appear very much in evidence - mass chaos, uncertainty, selfishness, lack of common sense, no respect for others, etc. The list of the "troubles" of the Sixties in all parts of the world is a long one. If one has the opportunity of "sitting back" and observing, it would appear as though the world and its people had gone mad. Of course, one can find no time in history when sages were not pointing out the same thing - that they were living in times of great trouble, chaos, selfishness, etc. However, it does seem that more than during most periods in world history, the Sixties provided man with an opportunity to overcome many of the great problems. Yet, man failed so miserably really to take advantage of newly discovered facts, developments, discoveries, technological knowledge, etc. which could have made for the greatest period in man's history. The failure to utilize the great discoveries of the recent past for the betterment of mankind and for the freeing of man from the shackles of mental enslavement is the great failure of the Sixties!

1

Of all the various failures in the Western World in our time there is none more dramatic, nor more senseless, than the failure of Judeo-Christian faiths to really relate the technological and psychological knowledge explosion to the basic spiritual needs of man. Never at any time in history has man had a greater opportunity to make the basic tenets of Christianity more meaningful and more useful to man. And what have the churches as a whole done? For the most part, nothing! They have merely told the younger generation to have "faith" and follow the dogma of the particular creed of their elders. As a result, which could be healthy for the modern church if a lesson is learned, the younger generation has looked at the church with some suspicion as it often seemed to refute the "new" knowledge; they have questioned the relevancy of the teachings to today's world; they have challenged the basics of Christianity *as given to them* by their dogmatic church. Never before has the Christian church had a greater opportunity to show the relevancy of the basic teachings of Jesus, the "oneness" of all the world's great religions, the very practical nature of all that is at the very basis of Christian teachings. Yet the church has ignored this opportunity! Hence, the younger people, with mockery in many cases, have turned to gurus (often of very dubious background) who have promised spiritual awakening; they have turned to various forms of sexual over-indulgence and promiscuity hoping to find some spiritual value there, turned to LSD and various other drugs which at times can be completely destructive - in fact, turned to almost anything that might give them a temporary spiritual up-lift; and they have found no lasting peace, no quietude, no answers to their basic human need for some spiritual experience and understanding.

Why do we in the Christian world express surprise when our youngsters seem to seek answers in all types of so called anti-social behavior? Could it be that much of this anti-social behavior falls into the category of "anti-social" because of the failure of society to establish any rational, Christian social behavior? Has there been too much hypocrisy in our churches? too much social-behavior rules dictated by dogma? too much emphasis on the "forbidden" rather than on the joyful experiences emphasized by Jesus? too much "hating" and not enough emphasis on Jesus' most important message, "loving"? Could our problems stem from the church failing to enlighten its members, let alone others, as to what can give real inner peace, real understanding, really meaningful relationships with others? Who among our church leaders has really tried to relate even a few of Jesus' or Buddha's, or Krishna's, or Mohammed's, or Confucius' teachings to each other? Have we shown the common roots and the relevancy of all the basic teachings to man in today's world? Are we not too concerned with our dogma, with our rules, with our ritual, with our lists of "sins"? *None* of our really great philosophers actually founded a church with rigid dogma - dogma that so often becomes much more important than the teaching upon which the church was founded!

The churches of the various religions came about through the efforts of later converts who were usually men of great goodwill and faith in the teachings of a spiritually enlightened "founder". However, dogma became the "thing" around which the institution was built rather than the teachings of the founder. Form and substance for the church were created from man-made and man-inspired rules rather than from spiritually enlightened teachings. The larger the institution (church) became the more important became the dogma. As in any organization change is resisted because of the fear of the unknown (the loss of security due to the change.) The rules (dogma) of the church (or any organization for that matter) became the "security blanket" for the administrators of the church and a change in rules was resisted more than change in almost any other area. Hence, dogma became very rigid and dominant. (There is nothing peculiar to churches in this respect. Any organization has to constantly guard against "rules" becoming the objectives or motives of the organization and has to keep constantly aware of the real objective of the organization.) Inevitably, unless careful precautions are taken, stagnation sets in. Often there seems to be the desire to preserve dogma even at the risk of the loss of the basic teachings of the original spiritual teacher who is the so-called founder of that particular church. Certainly, the usurping of the original objectives of the church by dogma is greatly in evidence in many (maybe most?) of our modern churches of all faiths.

One of the great events and one of the most healthy of the past decade was the calling of the Ecumenical Congress by Pope John. Why? It is through such a Congress that there is some hope of dogma being scrutinized, the organizational bind being loosened, questions of dogma being re-examined in light of the world in which the church now exists. Too bad the Ecumenical Congress could not have lasted longer, gone more deeply into the relevancy of much of the dogma, and found new ways of relating the church to the world today. Too bad that all churches - Protestant, Roman Catholic, Judaic, Greek Orthodox, Buddhist, Mohammedan, Hindu, etc. - do not constantly re-evaluate their work and rules and bring to current relevancy the basic teachings of their founders. After all the great spiritual truths never change - only the means by which man can understand and relate to those truths change. Man is too often trying to adjust spiritual truths to conform to rules and dogma - it is the rules and the dogma that should be changing to conform to new ways of teaching the great spiritual truths.

Because more freedom for the "priest" is allowed in Eastern religions and much less dogma exists, the Eastern "gurus" are often able to capture the imagination of our youth. A "mystique" grows up around them. The interest shown by the youth of Britain and the United States today in such a guru as Maharishi Mahesh, various Yogis and others of the Hindu and Buddhist persuasion is in large part due to greater freedom from dogma and much more emphasis on self-awareness and understanding by the "priests" of Eastern religions than by "priests" of Western religions. In the Western world we have allowed Freud and the psychiatrists to replace self-understanding and self-awareness. Interesting, too, how many of our Western formal church leaders complain about the lack of interest among young people in spiritual matters, or at least Christian church matters. Especially is this interesting when there is such strong evidence of the great interest of youth in spiritual understanding, which is manifested by the enthusiasm for Eastern gurus. But one should note how effectively the "gurus of the East" have communicated with youth - how dogma has been omitted or at least minimized. The Western religious leaders should have learned a great lesson, but did they?

4

Of all the failures of the Western religious leaders none seems more non-sensical and has less excuse than the failure to emphasize prayer and meditation and the benefits to be derived therefrom. Meditation and prayer are the very heart of Christianity! Today even modern science is able to demonstrate the tremendous power of meditation (see *Science,* March 17, 1970.) Why do so many of our youth assume that meditation is somehow foreign to Christianity? Why do they believe it is only in Eastern philosophies that meditation is taught? It is because our Christian churches have failed to relate to today's youth and have failed to emphasize the most important aspects and tenets of the Christian faith.

Practically all one hears concerning Maharishi and many of the other "gurus" of India relates to meditation. So many of the serious and well-intentioned young people, many of whom have had psychadelic experiences, want to experience serious meditation and have not been shown that it is an important aspect of progress for the practicing Christian. It were as though meditation was something entirely new to Western man. It is so difficult to understand why meditation, this basic teaching of Moses, Jesus, Paul and many other Judeo-Christian founders, seemingly is almost ignored by our Hebrew and Christian churches today. Yet the teachings - even the rituals - are full of the importance of meditation.

I am very much aware that the western churches preach of the need to meditate; but nothing important is done to show why meditation is essential, nothing is done to show the importance of meditation in learning to understand others ("turning-on Love"), in learning tolerance, in becoming more self-aware. We have had "best selling" books that are concerned with self-image building, in the power of thinking in a positive way, ways of self-hypnosis; but for the most part these books with all their appeal and good intent are not able to provide for lasting inner-peace and a building of goodwill among men *unless* consistent and daily concentration is practiced - concentration which is certainly a form of meditation.

Most of the "popular" Western religious leaders today - those who seem to attract the huge audiences and appear frequently on television - seem to still be primarily of the "fire and brimstone" type. However, they do seem to "spark" the imagination and bring people together in a temporary period of "spiritual ecstasy". It would be interesting to know for how long people affected by this sort of "preaching" feel peace, joy, harmony, in their lives! Most of our current "popular" religious teachers seem to believe that to "turn people on" requires a listing of sins (usually based on current thinking regarding anti-social behavior as defined by their own group) and the renouncing of sin. This is a far cry from the quiet and joy of meditation where man can become self-aware, far from Jesus' repeated statement that the "Kingdom of God is within," a far cry from helping man to be more sensitive and understanding of the weaknesses of others as well as his own. The youth of today is tired - and I would suspect so are the majority of the "oldsters" - of the constant preoccupation of organized religion and evangelists with sin. After all, Jesus never condemned and never was negative in his work or his words. Jesus preached a message of joy, of enthusiasm, of being "free" of sin. He did not have to forgive because he never condemned. Even the beginning student of psychology knows that man is motivated much more effectively and lastingly through the "positive" than through the "negative". Man is motivated through "freedom" rather than "fear" - at least he is more effectively motivated through concepts of freedom and the motivation stays with him much longer. Any individual who has done any work in advertising or counselling knows the importance of "reward" as contrasted to "punishment". But our evangelists and our churches continue to teach Christianity with "fear of God", "fear of fire and brimstone," and "fear of condemnation."

The preoccupation of Western religious leaders with the dogmatic admonitions of Paul and those who followed the strict Paulist doctrine has precluded instruction in meditation and has precluded the proper emphasis on those things which will really provide for man's spiritual needs. This is not to say that the Paulist doctine is wrong or is all negative; but rather that the negative and dogmatic aspects of Paul's teachings have been emphasized and the positive, affirmative teachings have been shamefully neglected. When one dwells on the negatives - the "thou shalt nots" - there is little opportunity for the positive. Above all else,

Christianity should be a "positive" type of religion - a faith to live with joy, enthusiasm and freedom! There is a great deal of difference between a "positive" type of faith and a "permissive" faith and this is where we have been so badly confused. There is little permissiveness in the teachings of the Eastern religious leaders - at least in those I have studied. But there is a great deal of the positive - the emphasis is on the beauty, the joy, the inner-peace, the brotherliness that comes through self-realization and enlightenment. Self-realization, they teach, is attained through meditation. Christianity emphasizes beauty, joy, inner-peace, self-realization, brotherliness *and* great permissiveness. Jesus taught that man has free will - that he can be master of his fate, that he has the right and ability to choose his destiny (at least from a spiritual sense.) Jesus told us in many ways of the importance of meditation, of the importance of self-awareness. Jesus gave us the way of going into the silence and finding God. However, by neglecting the positive aspects of Jesus' teachings and by neglecting what Jesus said about "free will" we have made Christianity seem both less permissive and less positive than Eastern teachings. Indeed, formal religious teachers and the evangelists frequently have made Christianity seem very restrictive, very authoritatian and very materialistic - all things that Christianity really *is not.*

The modern Christian church's emphasis on the "death on the cross" rather than on the "resurrection" and the emphasis on the sins of man rather than on the potential for good in man, etc. have made for a very negative religion which I believe is completely contrary to Jesus' objectives. When our medical men and psychologists are telling us and demonstrating to us the importance of positive thinking, how can we expect people to become enthused over a religion which emphasizes negative thinking? How wonderful it would be if Christian leaders would emphasize the story of the redemption of man, the story of rebirth, the story of the joy that comes through understanding oneself and others, the story of the ecstasy of seeing the beauty in all things - all very important aspects of Jesus' teachings! I believe we could create a real revolution in Western society if we would start relating the gospel of the glory of man and of Christ (of how through understanding

7

Jesus' teaching one can re-unite with pure Spirit) and stop placing the emphasis on the damnation of man, on the sins of man, on the evil in God's world! If we would start a program of teaching how to look for the "invisible in the visible," how to look for the good in all, how to see the purity in all things (of which Paul made such a point), how to discover our real selves, how to uncover the real purpose of life, then we would have a real Christian world around us and youth would be so attracted!

Both the Old and New Testament contain extremely interesting and important information on how to meditate, on the importance of self-realization, on the goodness of all creatures, on the need to respect and care for our natural environment. Most of our youngsters are completely ignorant of this information and they turn to esoteric religions, drugs, sex, astrology, witch-craft, etc. thinking that in these areas they may find the answer to the riddle of life. Whose fault is it that they turn to these off-beat and often harmful sources for information and help? I believe it is the fault of organized religion - it has failed to communicate the real message of Christianity and has chosen to communicate its own dogma. It has failed to follow the most basic rule in communicating - understand how the message to be sent will be seen through the "eyes" of the receiver.

In the chapter, "How the Victorious Spirit Can Come 'Alive' Within Man", I hope I effectively relate some of the scientific evidence of the validity of much that is within the Bible both in regard to the physical laws of nature and to the psychological aspects of man. However, none of this scientific evidence means anything and the breakthroughs in knowledge will still leave the West spiritually bankrupt if we continue on our "negativistic" course. The basic answer, of course, rests in learning to effectively meditate and coming to know the real purpose of life - to return to man's victorious Spirit (the Kingdom of God which is within.) The religious leaders still spilling "fire and brimstone" and "harping" on sin will have to do some serious revamping of their own thinking if the Christian religion is going to provide a meaningful spiritual home for most of today's Western world. How much better known and loved today is St. Francis, who dwelt on the world of beauty and found much of it through meditation, than are the men of the Inquisition who were preoccupied with sins and particularly sins relating to dogma! How much more effective in the long-run will be an Emmet Fox, a Pope John or a Peter Marshall than a modern theatrical "television-star" evangelist who threatens and who preaches fear! It is time - if not already too late - that our religious leaders relate to modern science and the great positive ministry of Jesus and forget the dogma and "sins" which have preoccupied them for so long. If they don't, they should not be surprised that few *really* will be interested in the churches (attendance may still be good because attendance is the "socially accepted" norm) but more and more of our youth will seek those teachers and those spiritual leaders outside organized religion who are not tied-down by dogma and the "negative." We should expect a turning away from Western churches and institutions unless the leaders start relating to the positive ministry of Jesus and the common roots of all religions. There will be a turning to those who are positive and loving in their approach to man's spiritual nature and man's capability.

When our religious teachers begin to realize that the great psychologist, Carl Jung, was right when he theorized that man's great drive is for life and for finding meaning in life, then these "religionists" may begin to teach in a manner which will be meaningful to man. When we are aided by our churches in finding our way back to pure Spirit, the churches will become highly relevant. We *are not aided* by being told what not to do and being threatened with dire punishment if we do certain things. We *are aided* when we are told *what to do* in order to more joyously, more peacefully, more harmoniously find our way back to pure Spirit - a way to walk the road of life with God.

CHAPTER TWO

Man's Self-Image and the Divine Nature
of Man

Today most people know enough of psychology to talk rather actively of "personality blocks", of inhibitions, of "Freudian slips", of the "images we hold" of "masks that we wear", of "games that we play", etc. However, most of us do not know about or even vaguely realize that the greatest psychological problem faced by man is the image that man has of himself. I am talking about man in the collective sense rather than in the singular. We seem to hold the image of man as that of an independent being, of a creature superior to all other creatures here on Earth, of a "thinking" and highly rational entity. Most of these "collective" images are far from correct. In many respects man is the most irrational of all entities, the most irresponsible of all beings. It may well be that man is the least intuitive, the most emotionally driven, and the most irresponsible of all creatures. No other creature kills his own, no other creature is so interdependent within his own kind, no other creature ignores nature - indeed, destroys his natural environment. However, *all* of these negative aspects of man *do not have to be.* From the standpoint of the ability to think creatively man *is* superior to all other beings. From the standpoint of being able to truly understand his intuition and his instinct man is superior. Since man appears to be the only creature with true emotions (although that is far from being proved scientifically), it should be true that man can govern those emotions through his intellect. However, most men permit their emotions to govern them. Man emerges from any type

10

of comparative analysis with most other creatures as a pretty poor being - at least as far as his ecological awareness and his understanding of his fellow creatures are concerned.

What has happened to mankind that has created this vacuum in his awareness of his fellow man and the Earth on which he lives and depends? I believe it is due to his own lack of awareness of his purpose for being on Earth. I believe it stems from a lack of a sense of direction within man. Some few great men throughout history appear to have possessed a keen sense of direction in regard to why man is on Earth. These men have not all been great philosophers or great theologians or great psychologists. Many have been in very humble jobs and have been very humble people. They have been men without "personality blocks." If man is truly to find his way out of the morass of problems he has created in his world, he must begin to have faith in himself. He must start building an image that is far different than the collective image of man held today. *And* this will begin with individual man developing a realistic self-image. A self-image not based on emotions but based on reason - pure reason!

Most of our problems stem from a lack of faith in ourselves - a lack of faith because we lack inner-direction. We lack faith in ourselves because we have built up false images of ourselves - we conform to the image we hold of ourselves and if the image is false naturally our thought and action will be false. Only the truth about ourselves will permit us to construct the image that we must have - a rational image based on a strong goal.

If one's life is based on that which is without, then how can one come to know that which is within? If we construct our goals, if we build our images only on the external - the material - how can we hope to know what our true potential is? How can we ever know our attributes, our strenghs, our intuitive creative ability, if we have only examined our external conditions and believe only what has been told us about ourselves by others and by our environment? Obviously each individual will have an image of himself dictated to him by others and by his environment if he only looks without. Is this a rational method of determining what we are? I submit that this is the most irrational way in which to construct our self-image.

Man, because of his ability to live in a world of illusion, frequently cannot see his own motives. Because he lives only for the material aspects of the world and creates his image of himself and others from the world as understood by his sensory system only, he lives under a very real illusion as to what he really is, of what his goals truly should be, of what he can accomplish. Dr. Maxwell Maltz says in *Psycho-Cybernetics* that if man allows himself to believe whatever is told him often enough, that becomes his reality concerning himself.

It is strange how man will seek out prophets and seers, fortune tellers, card readers, etc. to tell him his destiny! If one wants prophecies or messages he can pick up the Bible. There is a great deal of prophecy there and a great many messages as personally directed to each of us as any message could be. But none of the messages - Biblical or otherwise - means anything if one is looking to the outside for the meaning of the message. Look to the prophecy or the message for the means, or the channel, or a way, but do *not* look at it as the end - *the* way. If one looks at prophecy or at a message (from the Bible or from psychic sources) as the end (*the* way) it becomes the *escape* - one begins to assume when this happens or that arrives everything will be o.k. Only a man who has reached "Christ Consciousness" or has come into union with the victorious Spirit can "call his own shots" - he must have complete faith and reliance on the victorious Spirit which is within himself. We are not conscious of the Spirit until we have come into spiritual enlightenment. If all answers were provided through prophecy or through "messages", no matter what the source, we would lose our initiative, our prod - the electric shock - that keeps us going forward. We would lose all motivation if we knew the future - we probably would come to the point of saying "what is to be, is to be" or "it is God's will and it will be done." Probably the worst thing that could happen to us would be for us to become aware of our future and just how that future was to come about. Certainly the mystery and drama of life would be missing! What really is important is that the effort to make the climb or to overcome the problem would not be exerted. Certainly, too, as Paul tells us in I Corinthians 14:1-5, "Put love first; but there are other gifts of the spirit at which you should aim also, and above all prophecy. When a man is using the language of ecstasy he is talking to God, not with men, for no man understands him; he is no doubt inspired, but he speaks in mysteries. On the other hand, when a man prophesies, he is talking to men, and his words have power to build; they stimulate and encourage. The language of ecstasy is good for the speaker himself, but it is prophecy that builds up a Christian community. I should be pleased for you all to use the tongues of ecstasy, but better pleased for you to prophesy. The prophet is worth more than the man of ecstatic speech."

I believe Paul was thinking of prophecy more in the preferred dictionary meaning - "to utter by divine inspiration." Hence, it is not apt to be the same thing as fortune telling. A real prophet will give us divine inspiration to go forward. He may hold out certain things for us but he does not tell us that certain things *will* necessarily happen. He inspires us to try to make, or not make, them happen.

We should realize that much of the prophecy of this world is purely of a worldly nature - when we will get this, when we will do that, when a certain event will occur, etc. This is of no lasting value; and as an aid to us in achieving a sense of worth - to build a better self-image or to find meaning in our existence - it is valueless. In fact, this materialistic type of prophecy may really be quite destructive for us because it may delay our search for the real meaning of life and delay the activation of the desire to understand ourselves.

When man chose to be born he broke his bond with pure Spirit - he became separated from the pure Spirit of God. Man chose to come into the Earth incarnation in order to work out certain problems that existed within his particular soul. There is a price to be paid in working this out but the objective is to *return to pure Spirit with pure Spirit*. This is the answer to man's search for meaning in life - it is to make our soul's totality once again unite with pure Spirit from which it was separated at birth. Perhaps this is the meaning of "original sin" - we broke away from pure Spirit when we were born. The objective of life is to meet our problems in as spiritual a manner as possible so that we can return to the pure Spirit from which we were divided. In a sense, the "sin" is in being born because it took us away from pure Spirit and we are incomplete. We are not "impure" because we are a part of pure Spirit - we broke away - but we are not complete because we are a separated part. The meaning of life for man is to return to the total victorious Spirit of which man's spirit is a separated part. As I develop later in this book, "the spirit that was divided will be united; Love will stay united yet will be divided to be given to the still divided spirits that all will be united."

Man must learn to drop whatever he has created which keeps him from the greater force - his victorious Spirit. Man cannot find meaning in life without knowing self; he cannot know self until he knows what self is a part of; he cannot know what self is a part of until he knows from what self was separated. When he truly knows that it was from pure Spirit that he was separated and that he is a separated part of pure Spirit, then life takes on meaning and his own evaluation of himself - his own self-image - becomes a very beautiful thing (and a highly motivating factor in his future growth.) Man begins to see the great beauty that is within himself and all his fellow men! He can experience the ecstasy of knowing that all are simply separated parts of pure Spirit - that purity, good, love are everywhere! However, this knowledge of the meaning of life, this knowledge of the beauty and purity everywhere will not come about through dwelling on worldly things, through relying on mediums to tell us what is going to happen to us. It requires that man cease living in a world of illusion which he calls "reality" and start living in the real world - the world of self-awareness and God-awareness. Again, if one's life is based on that which is without how can one come to know that which is within?

Man has to realize that he is *not* here on Earth to fulfill some worldly ambition, some worldly plan, to achieve something of a worldly nature. He is not here to become a doctor, a lawyer, a farmer, a professor, a humanitarian, a writer - man's purpose for his incarnation is to return home! It is to rise in consciousness to the point where he is no longer separated from Spirit (from God if one prefers.) Worldly prophecy will not aid man one iota in learning how to become reunited with pure Spirit. Only through his effort to understand and practice love, no matter in what walk of life or in what circumstances he finds himself, can man return to his great victorious Spirit from which he was separated. Man can always call upon that Spirit for aid, for assistance, for comfort and for sustenance; but man must do the calling *on his own initiative.* But man must never, ever, sever his consciousness from the realization that he is not here just to be "something" in the sense of a position or job - he must maintain in his consciousness the fact he is here to find his way home again, back to pure Spirit. However, isn't it true that most of us have severed our consciousness from any desire to return to pure Spirit? Haven't we ignored this entire aspect of ourselves? Indeed, haven't we normally not even considered this fundamental need we have? We have become completely involved with seeking positions in life, with seeking creature comfort, with seeking power, fame and worldly glory. We have become "blinded by the gods of this passing age" and we have missed the beauty, the love and the ecstasy which comes from seeking our reunification with victorious Spirit!

One cannot make the attempt to "return home to pure Spirit from which one has been separated" and prepare for something else at the same time. We are too constantly preparing ourselves for "something else". We are always "gearing" ourselves in preparation for something else. Yet, we so seldom know for what we are truly preparing. We should ask ourselves, "I am preparing for something, what am I preparing for?" In the midst of our trying to find a meaning to life, a way out of a problem, a way to establish a relationship, etc. we usually are preparing for something else as well. How can one be still, how can one be at "home with oneself" when one is preparing to go somewhere or do something else? When we are trying to do something and prepare for something else (often, we know not what), the mind is split. When the mind is split how can the creative energy be directed in the *one* place? It cannot be so directed because where the mind is split it must be divided - it must be diffused - and then one is left with the emotions. Because one cannot make a right turn and a left turn at the same time, there is a stoppage - a ceasing of any progress unless one finally concentrates on

15

either the right or left turn and does not continue to prepare for the other turn. If man is truly to come into harmony with this world, if man is to feel truly at ease, if man is truly to experience love, he must concentrate on the true meaning of life - the return to pure Spirit - and cease his constant preparation for this or that other activity. This does *not* mean that man must cease his attempts to become professional at whatever work he is doing or aspires to do. This does *not* mean that man must cease his preparation to solve and work with the problems of this world. What it does mean is that man *must* cease to see the problem, the job as *the* objective, as *the* preparation; and he must come into the realization that the only *real* objective is the return home to pure Spirit from which he has been separated. When he realizes that, he will quit dividing himself - diffusing his creative force - and be able to concentrate with all his creative energy on his "preparation" in a meaningful and effective way. Today man is so divided, is preparing for so many "things", that he does not really prepare for anything! We must cease living in the world of illusion with its constant preparation which has no inner sense of direction. We must have a deep understanding of what all ultimate preparation is for - the return to pure Spirit. Then the tasks of this world, the problems of this world can be handled with great effectiveness. We must have a collective goal - a sense of meaning of life - or all of our energy and *our creative force* become diffused through constant preparation. Without an understanding of what we are preparing for we stand still - we can move neither to the right nor to the left.

When one examines the world situation today it becomes very obvious that man, in the collective sense, has no goal - no meaningful objective. Hence, man is constantly "preparing for peace", "preparing for war", "preparing for changing economic conditions", "preparing to handle some new social problem", etc. The preparation becomes so meaningless because the central goal is missing - there is no real meaning of a lasting nature in the preparation because most men have no ever-lasting goal. When man realizes and *really* believes that the real purpose of life is to reunite with pure Spirit then he has a meaningful goal which becomes his basic preparation. It becomes basic to everything he does - his job, his profession, his problem-solving, his everyday activities. He then does not diffuse his preparation, does not divide his creative energy - his preparation for the reuniting with Spirit becomes very much a part of his everyday activities. He then can truly become a man who is divinely inspired, a man who has great creative energy, a man who is not divided. He becomes a man with a mission - a meaningful goal.

I take great exception to the admonition, "prepare for the second coming of Christ." How does one prepare for the coming of the savior, of a teacher, of a guru, or whatever? How would one prepare? It is as though you are to become so fearful with your way of life, so frightened, so threatened, that you become "good" to gain favor in the eyes of the great one. Isn't that bargaining? There is only one way to prepare for "the second coming of Christ" as there is only one way to prepare for finding the meaning to life. That way is to bring your consciousness - your entire being - into the stream of energy that leads to the reuniting of yourself with the all victorious Spirit from which you have been separated. If one truly holds to what is his purpose in this Earth incarnation he is prepared for anything - any problem, any profession for which he is trained, for any job and, certainly, for the "second coming of Christ." Special preparation is not necessary for the meeting of anyone or anything *if* one has focused on the only real preparation - reuniting with pure Spirit.

We should look closely at our prayers and our meditation. Quite often our prayers and meditation form a kind of bargaining time instead of a time to come back to Spirit. In our prayers don't we often make strong statements that we will try to do more of this and cast more light on the suffering world if only Spirit will give us a little more help? How many times in our meditation have we offered ourselves to the creative force and said, "what can I do for you and how may I help you?" Looking at our prayers and meditation in this manner becomes rather embarrassing to most of us! We seldom, if ever, truly offer ourselves - we usually offer to be of assistance only in the bargaining sense (only if we are given something - usually of a material nature.) In our prayers we often talk about how we may be of help, how we may be a channel to or for someone. Quite often our motive is highly suspect - if we examine the motive! How often the motive behind offering to help, to be a channel of assistance, etc. is highly selfish, highly materialistic! However, in prayer and meditation, communion with God (Holy Communion), don't try to ask God to be a kind of "divine bellhop". Examine your motive for the various requests you make; and if your motive is truly unselfish, truly loving, make no preparation. Don't try to prepare or make yourself ready to do something outside of yourself. Let go! Be willing to let the accumulated thoughts and ideas drop one by one from you so that you may first of all unite with the inner, so that you then may truly *be* instead of *becoming* or preparing for. If you *are,* then there is no preparation for what you will be. You probably never can know for certain when you are and that is good. Because when you think you are you are not. *But* it is that commitment, that willingness, that desire, to let go and to be as one with nature, with life, with love, whatever it may be - it is that commitment which must precede all or all else is doomed to fail. We must realize the importance of the expression, *I am.* In that expression I recognize that I *am* and there is no longer the emphasis on "what will I become." There is no longer the need for the preparation which stands in the way of uniting with the pure Spirit from which we are separated.

Since we are created in perfect love and in perfection and then we separate from what we are, the gap of the separation can be, and usually is, widened by the personality trying to perfect that which is already perfect. The personality is the "outer self" - it is the image created by an individual through his sensory system. It matters not what affected the sensory system - education, environment, experience, etc. - personality is still created from the "outer world", and is not a product of "inner understanding." Dwelling on the personality can only widen the gap of the separation between our creation in perfect love, in perfection, and our worldly idea of perfecting the worldly image. Most of us are trying to make something within us a little bit purer, a little bit whiter, a little bit more loving, a little bit closer to what we call God. How foolish it is when it *is* already perfect! As Paul states in Romans 14:14, "I am absolutely convinced, as a Christian, that nothing is impure in itself; only, if a man considers a particular thing impure, then to him it is impure." Certainly Paul is telling us that we are already pure and only our concept of ourselves as impure can create the impurity.

We cannot see that something is perfect unless we are willing to look at it; but we are so busy assuming that what we look at will not be perfect that we hastily throw changes around similar to changes of clothing! Yet we never really have looked, never really evaluated the situation! We have been content with the illusion world in which we live and then we wonder why we do not find answers to the "riddle of life." We have failed to understand that each of us is created in perfection and is fully created, *is!* We are constantly preparing *to become.* The perfection is there - perfection in being, in concepts, in love, in harmony, in answers.

The imperfection of today's world and within us has come about through allowing the personality, the "worldly" image of ourselves, to create the illusion of imperfection. Hence, until man is willing to realize that he is created in perfection and is simply a separated part of perfection, man will keep right on preparing for certain events and certain situations and he will find no peace. Man *must* start the search for seeing the perfection within himself and others - what better description of love than the art of looking for perfection within oneself and others? When man begins to see this perfection - this love - then truly the chaotic state in which he finds himself will be corrected and man will truly find inner peace and inner joy. This discovery will manifest itself in outer conditions making for outer peace and outer joy along with the inner. Finding perfection is not an impossible dream nor an illusion. It is the only reality and the world's present method of viewing man and all creation is the illusion! When an individual knows that his reason for existence is to find the way home to victorious Spirit and that all was created in perfection, he then finds peace and meaningful answers to life's problems.

Plants seek the sun, the river the sea, the seed the soil - all seek the source of their being. Only man looking to the moment distorts his true goal. The moment looms so large in front of him it blinds him to the greater, grander goal of Spirit. But what a wonderous and meaningful moment

19

when man becomes aware of the source of his being and
starts on the homeward voyage!

CHAPTER THREE

How the Victorious Spirit Can Come "Alive" Within Man

One hears so much about the word "relevant" today but one so seldom relates it to Christianity or to developing "Spirit" so that Spirit can play a part in one's everyday life. In fact, many people are saying that Christianity is so non-relevant to today's world that "God is dead." This is utter nonsense - yet, there is an element of truth in the statement, "God is dead," *because* we have failed to understand the great, basic teachings of Jesus and have failed to make those teachings relevant to today's language, to today's scientific information and to today's world. We have not tried to see the great relevancy to today's world and the situation of man today with what the great spiritual teachers have taught. We have left Spirit out of problem solving and then wondered why we find such chaos amongst us when so much technical and scientific information is readily available. We keep wondering why there is so little joy and peace in the world when man has made such gigantic progress in technical areas. Sometimes one is a little startled to realize how much *more* joy and peace there still seems to be in some parts of the world where technical and scientific progress have been minimal compared to the industrial areas. Could it be that these "backward" or "emerging" peoples know something about Spirit we don't know? Perhaps they are not as blinded by the "gods of the passing age" as we are. Isn't it time that we took this magnificent technical and scientific progress and related *it* to man's Spirit? Is this so unrealistic? Haven't we always said that man does not live by bread alone? Aren't we trying to live "by bread alone" when we develop only one leg

21

of the trinity - mind, body and spirit? If one observes a three-legged stool (such as a milking stool) it quickly becomes evident that the stool cannot stand with one leg missing - it cannot be balanced no matter how one strives to make it so. Man is very much as this stool in regard to developing his three aspects - body, mind and spirit. No wonder man feels so hemmed in, cut off, alienated today - he is trying to stand on one or two legs when he can only achieve balance when all three are developed. It is only when Spirit is released along with mind and body that man becomes balanced, that man can feel at peace with himself and with those around him. Emphasis on the equal development of the three aspects of man would make Christianity very relevant, and it *is* relevant because man must develop all three aspects if he is to survive and to achieve even a minimum of peace while surviving. The one thing man seeks - whether he recognizes it or not - is a reason for living. It is in Spirit that this reason for living will be found. How could anything be more relevant?

We need to interpret meanings within the great teachings of Jesus or (for that matter) within the teachings of any of the great teachers of any religion. Even within science we must interpret meanings of the great scientists of the past (are not scientists still working on ideas of Einstein, even of Leonardo?) We should attempt to interpret the meanings of scripture just as we do with meanings behind many of our great authors of the past and present. How many of our great universities today present in the ordinary liberal arts program an interpretation of the scriptures of any religion? However, most of them have numerous courses offered on Shakespeare, Dante, Dickens, etc. - even such modern day writers as Mailer, Jones and Hemingway! Are the minor works of Shakespeare more full of meaning or more beautifully written than John or I Corinthians? Are the modern writers more relevant than Revelations or Isaiah? They are not *as relevant!* However, we fail to interpret the scriptures in terms of today's knowledge and with the understanding that all great teachers must use the language, the stories, the parables that are in current usage amongst the people with whom they are working. We have to realize that Jesus, his disciples and the great teachers that preceded Jesus, were all working with a highly illiterate, highly volatile, highly unsophisticated people. All had to use words, symbols, stories, etc. that were pertinent to and understood by the people with whom they were working. Our first step in making Christianity relevant is to realize that we must interpret the words of scripture in terms of today - the message is there for us even though it is cloaked in symbols, words and stories more clearly understood two thousand years ago. With our understanding today of semantics, symbology (especially as explained by Carl Jung), parables, etc. we should find Christian teachings highly pertinent and very meaningful in guiding us toward solutions for our current problems.

For many of this generation there are many references in the Bible, particularly in the Old Testament, that seem far-fetched, unrelated to Truth, either from the scientific viewpoint or from the very basic premise that "God is love." Yet many of these references that literally "turn us off" could, in the light of modern knowledge, strengthen and solidify for us the Truth that the Bible really holds. Few of us understand the necessity for the leaders of the ancient world to speak in nonscientific terms. We fail to recognize the great principle of all really effective teaching: using the language and the figures of speech that are understandable to the people who are being taught. The people of two or three thousand years ago were for the most part illiterate, nomadic, easily moved by signs and portents. Certainly they had no knowledge of atomic energy, nuclear fission, or even the most rudimentary information concerning electrical energy.

In my own study of the Bible, one particular passage - the twenty-sixth verse of the nineteenth chapter of Genesis - had always struck me as particularly unrealistic, the opposite of the concept of God as love and contrary to nature. The verse reads, "But Lot's wife behind him looked back, and she became a pillar of salt." (When Lot was to lead his family out of Sodom and Gomorrah to the small city of Zoar, he was admonished to allow no one to look back, lest he be turned into a pillar of salt.) It is hard to see why a God of love would destroy Lot's wife for looking back. And why turn his wife into a pillar of salt? Why not a pillar of sand, into brimstone, into a plant, into a stake? Why, indeed, turn her into anything? What was the purpose, what was accomplished except to show the power, (perhaps even the avarice), of an all-powerful God?

Of course I have no basic answer as to why Lot's wife

became a pillar of salt, if indeed she did. I can speculate on the culture of the people at that time and the immense importance that was attached to salt (it was used as a preservative, as a sacrifice, it symbolized hospitality, durability, and purity). However, even knowing the importance of salt to the ancient Hebrew culture does not give us any real feeling for the symbology that must be expressed in the phrase "she became a pillar of salt."

However, if we apply some of our scientific knowledge to what we know of salt and what we know of "mind action," perhaps we can see the true significance of this story of Lot and his wife. It is now a well-established scientific fact that energy, unused, crystallizes. We know that salt is a crystalline substance. We know what happens to a flashlight battery (or any battery, for that matter) that is unused. Crystals begin to form around the chemical ingredients and the battery becomes powerless, a "heap of useless chemicals." Perhaps what the story of Lot's wife signifies is this: If we continually look back, dwell on the past, on past mistakes, on old ideas and concepts, if we refuse to keep our eyes and mind on the beauty of the future, the potential for growth and understanding that lies ahead, we are going to stagnate. By dwelling on the past (looking toward the past), we are crystallizing our energy and our ability to progress; we are turning our energy field into a "pillar of salt." Whether or not this is the meaning behind the Biblical story, it is still a powerful lesson for us. How many of us spend our time and our energy dwelling on past mistakes, past opportunities overlooked, past misfortunes! How few of us keep our eye on the potentials for growth and beauty in the future!

There is further evidence of the truth that is buried in the story of Lot's wife. The Metaphysical Bible Dictionary says: "When we remember the pleasures of the senses, and long for their return, we preserve the sense desire. This desire will manifest somewhere, sometime, unless the memory is dissolved through renunciation."

Recently I had the privilege of seeing again the great motion picture "Gone With the Wind." Again I was struck by the destruction that Scarlett O'Hara brought upon herself by continually looking back, by dwelling on the past beauty of Tara, the love she felt as a girl for Ashley, her inability to recognize change in both herself and in Ashley. Think of the opportunities she missed for happiness, both in terms of her family and in terms of her relationship with Rhett Butler! She was expending her energy in trying to rectify (or control) the mistake she felt both Ashley and she had made years before. If she had not been "looking over her shoulder" to the past, she could have had everything she had ever wanted and more, in her relationship with Melanie and Rhett. Margaret Mitchell must have had a great understanding of the basic Truth principle that joy and happiness exist in the present and future and not in the past.

How many of the passages of the Bible, particularly in the Old Testament, are fraught with great wisdom and truth for us, if we would only take the time to speculate concerning the meaning within these parables and stories! How fascinating both science and Biblical literature can become if we are willing to look behind the literal words that are used! We must keep in mind that all the great teachers have used and use words, symbols, objects well known to their audiences - today, or three thousand years ago. It is surely not mere coincidence that similar stories concerning such things as a "pillar of salt" appear in almost all the scriptures of all the world's great religions. Truth is the same no matter what cloak it is given.

Whether or not the great spiritual teachers had knowledge of salt being crystalline substance, whether or not they had any knowledge of the energy force of thought - these things are immaterial. There was certainly symbolic significance attached to a "pillar of salt" in ancient times. The truth of the fact that one cannot develop energy by dwelling on past negatives can be demonstrated today in the scientific laboratory. The fact that unused energy does crystallize is something even the junior-high-school student knows. For me, the great lesson that is "hidden" in the passage concerning Lot and his wife is this: When I dwell on the past (look over my shoulder), I am destroying my own ability to progress, to grow, and to understand - an ability that God has given to me, as He has to everyone who cares to look ahead and see the potential for growth, keeping eyes and mind on the beauty of the future and not on the evils of the past.

God may be dead to many because He is dead to anyone *if* one has not developed his spirit faculty - has not started on the road to God. We must realize that we create our own reality - nothing has meaning to us or for us until we have developed a frame of reference toward it. In other words, nothing exists for us until we create it. Hence, God never comes to life for us unless we have developed a frame of reference toward Spirit or God, if that term is preferable. If one has never attempted to develop an attitude toward Spirit, Spirit does not exist for him. As an example, if I had never developed a frame of reference in regard to "door", "door" does not exist for me and for me it would be as though "door" never existed. "Door" would be dead because it had never come alive for me. If one never attempts to develop an attitude toward God - never looks for God's existence - then God is dead and will be dead until a frame of reference or attitude is formed.

Another reason for the seeming lack of relevancy of Christianity to today's world is that man has failed to live the Christian life; and therefore, Christianity has not been relevant. *Nothing* has meaning (or is relevant) unless it is put to use or appears to one's consciousness. George Bernard Shaw once said that the only trouble with Christianity was that it had never been tried (this could so easily be said of all the great religions of the world - so few people have tried to *live the life* expounded to them!) Of course to live a Christian life one must know what a Christian life is and understand the lessons given the world by Jesus. The central core of all of Jesus' teachings - and the teachings of all the great religions of the world without exception - is love. And how little our world understands love! There is so much in science, particularly in medical science, to explain the importance of love - there is so much proof of what Jesus was teaching. Yet, man has gone on some very real tangents in regard to the meaning of love. There is Hollywood's version of love - pure physical attraction; there is some financiers' version of love - pure materialism, etc. etc. Actually Hollywood and the financiers are probably talking about lust and greed which are about as far apart as anything can be from love. I will discuss love in some detail in Chapter 8, but at this point I wish to point out that Paul in I Corinthians 13:1-13 expresses love's meaning just about perfectly. (This New Testament passage appears in Chapter 8.)

Medical science has shown in so many ways the destrucive power of hate and the building power of love. For example, it is now known that ulcers are primarily caused by worry or hatred. Nothing is much more destructive to a man trying to cope with a difficult person or problem than an ulcer - he is really incapacitated. Yet, worry and/or hatred are the primary cause of ulcers. Christians are told that hate kills the hater and that the only practical thing one can do when faced with an enemy is to love him! Now we know through scientific demonstration that hating harms the hater and not the hated! We know that love gives us the energy to cope with the situation. Every human being is able to demonstrate man's victorious Spirit!

One might say that worry has very little to do with hatred. On the contrary, worry has a great deal to do with hatred. Worry is quite contrary to *all* Christian teachings. When one analyzes worry one finds that it is fear of failure to successfully deal with a situation. This means there is self-doubt (lack of love of oneself) and/ or lack of faith in Spirit's victoriousness. In any manner in which one looks at "worry" one finds that it is the very antithesis of love and it is definitely contrary to Christ's teachings.

There have been so many studies by scientists of great renown concerning the power of the mind over the body that sometimes one almost wonders if Phineas Quimby is back with us! Yet, these men who are not primarily religious leaders are bearing witness to the tremendous power of the mind to control body functions. This of course comes as no surprise to an individual who has studied Christian teachings.

There have been demonstrations under laboratory conditions of the power of deep meditation to affect the actual flow of blood within the body and to change the entire body metabolism. The stronger the exercise of love the stronger has been the meditation - in this case, love has been equated with faith in oneself to find God (Spirit). There is so much more to say about love that much will have to be said in a later chapter, but it is the most important of the "relevancy" points for today's living.

Dr. Joshua Lederberg, the famed Nobel Prize Winner, has cited experiments where blood flow from one side of the body to the other was directed by the mind; Dr. Shafica Karagulla in her magnificent book, *Breakthrough to Creativity,* has given example after example of psychic awareness - of awareness of illness and/or forthcoming illness in others; Dr. Andreja Puharich has presented scientific proof

27

of the remarkable healing ability of Arigo of Brazil. These physicians, and many others, have given great testimony of the power of the thought-force of the mind over the body. Certainly we have been told about this in Christianity. We have been told, "As a man thinketh in his heart so is he." Christ said in John 14:12: "In truth in very truth I tell you, he who has faith in me will do what I am doing and he will do greater things still."

We should not look upon the healing miracles of scripture as isolated incidents and impractical. Certainly the healing cited in the Bible has great basis in scientific fact which is now being demonstrated in many of the world's leading scientific laboratories - again, the power of the mind over matter (one energy force over another) can now be proven! One should remember what St. Augustine said, "Miracles are not contrary to nature, only contrary to what we know about nature."

I have had many tell me that they cannot believe in the concept which holds that there is power in thought. Their reason for this inability to comprehend or accept the idea of "invisible power" normally appears to be that they cannot detect the power through their sensory system. My answer is, "How often have you seen the power that runs your car through gasoline, or the power that lies within the electric lines into your home (indeed, seen electricity), or the power that rests in steam?" None of us actually sees "power", we only see the result of the action of power. A little searching will reveal great manifestations of the power of the mind in governing the action and reaction of the body. When the potential power of the mind is combined with the great power of Spirit (which we "turn on" through meditation and/or prayer) there is no limit to what can be accomplished. I like to recall what Albert Schweitzer had to say about "invisible power": "The power of ideals is incalculable. We see no power in a drop of water. But let it get into a crack in the rock and be turned into ice, and it splits the rock; turned into steam it drives the pistons of the most powerful engines. Something has happened to it which makes active and effective the power that is latent in it."

I believe that man has very often so misinterpreted, misunderstood, or so dramatically changed the intent and meaning of scripture that Christianity has frequently been used in a way absolutely the opposite of its true objectives.

28

Certainly no one has to cite the destruction levied upon many by so-called Christians during the Crusades and the Inquisition. However, one finds even today many mis-guided individuals using words from scripture to excuse the most inhumane of acts and the cruelest of hoaxes.

In speaking of going forth into all the nations and peoples of the world with his message, could Jesus have been talking about the multiplying power of love? It would be the easiest way to reach all nations and people *and* love was the basic message of Jesus. He told us again and again to let your light so shine forth that all will know you as a follower of Christ Consciousness. People full of love *do* radiate energy which is light and heat - the auric colors revealed to some certainly give great witness to the increasing intensity of light around those who manifest love in thought as well as action. Dr. Karagulla has demonstrated this so well in her book, *Breakthrough to Creativity*. The power of love is much more powerful than the power of positive thinking. Positive thinking is very helpful; and as a matter of fact, it is very important but without love it is not nearly as effective as it could be.

Have we ever realized that potentially the greatest revolution man has ever seen - or ever could see - is possible through the exercise of love? Jesus lived thirty-three years on earth. According to computations which are supported by computer analysis, if one were able to find one other person this year with whom he could express perfect love, next year that person found another and the original man found another; and each year thereafter each found one more, after thirty-two years one half of the world would have been affected - the thirty-third year the entire world would have been reached! Is this what Jesus really meant when he talked about going forth into all nations? Is this what is meant by letting "your light so shine forth?" Certainly individuals who have great love in their hearts do radiate great light, energy, warmth.

There are many concepts of Christianity that one should think about in establishing a "mode of living." There are so many guidelines that would make life so much more full of meaning and would truly make relevant to today's living the practice of Christianity. Here are just a few ideas or "pointers" which might serve as such guidelines and each will be discussed more fully later: the magnificent work done by the Jungian psychologists concerning the "image" world we create which becomes our reality; the need of man to understand that he is a part of the "oneness" of all men but is, at the same time, unique; the fact that our nervous system cannot tell the difference between what we vividly imagine and what is reality; the absolute power of our thoughts to control *every* aspect of our lives including our body.

In both the Old and New Testaments the importance of prayer (meditation - silence) is stressed. How many conscientiously pray and understand what silent meditation and prayer can do both mentally and physically to say nothing about what meditation and prayer do to the spiritual aspects of man? Jungian psychologists have pointed out to us the importance of focusing on good, the importance of looking for good in all things. Many years ago Emerson told us that mental health was the propensity to find good in everything. When we dwell on the negative - the evil we see in people and things - we certainly are not dwelling on the "good". We are focusing our mind on the negative which is the same as hatred and worry in its effect on the body and mind. When one is dwelling in silence, in prayer, in meditation one dwells on "good" and leaves the negative aside - that is, if one really understands how to pray and the meaning of prayer. How often we try to make God a kind of "divine bellhop" and try to tell Him what to do! How often our prayers are devoted to pure materialism. How seldom we let go and let God! Jung tells us that man's basic drive is a search for meaning in life - that this is man's great drive and man's true motivating force. It is in prayer (or meditation, or dwelling in the silence, or going into the wilderness) that man can find real meaning for living. We must realize that it is a scientific fact that our nervous system and brain cannot tell the difference between what we vividly imagine to be true and what is reality. Hence, in our prayers, in our meditation, we must dwell on the good, we must form the habit of looking for the good in all things. Very basic to Christianity is the admonition that thinking of doing the act is the same in many respects as doing the act. Psychology certainly confirms this - if we vividly imagine anything enough it becomes a reality to us (our brain and nervous system cannot tell the difference.)

We must begin to realize the very great importance - and

relevancy to today's living - of developing the three sides of man - mind, body and spirit (the Holy Trinity?)

To make relevant today the practice of Christianity all we have to do is to use what we have been taught through Christian teachings and what we know intuitively!

It will help in relating Christianity to the modern world to realize how very wise with *scientific* wisdom have been the great spiritual teachers. However, so often we have distorted what they have taught because of dogmatic creeds that have become *the* beliefs of many of the church leaders. Let us look at a few of the scientific facts now established which were in the scriptures but were ignored, even denied, by dogmatic church leaders.

In Isaiah 40:22 we find a description that would indicate the world is round - only the medieval church refused to look at this passage except from a dogmatic standpoint and so the Judaic-Christian churches were thought to be unscientific when it was discovered the world was round.

In many passages (Exodus 34:22, I Samuel 1:20, II Chronicles 24:23, Job 38:12-14) it is revealed that the earth revolves around the sun. However, the church chose to interpret these passages differently to conform to dogma with the result that when Copernicus made his "discovery" that the earth revolved around the sun he was condemned and hounded by the church as being anti-scripture.

In Job 26:7 and Job 38:4,6 there are references which could easily be interpreted as explaining scientific laws of gravity and the laws of centrifugal force and motion. These were set down thousands of years before Newton! Again, they were denied by the dogmatic church leaders.

The science dealing with weather (meteorology) is a relatively recently developed science. Yet, there are numerous references in the scriptures concerning this field - much now confirmed by science. Especially in Jeremiah 10:13 and Ecclesiastes 1:6-7 one finds very pointed references which would have been of aid to man hundreds of years ago in his study of meteorology if man had chosen to look at scripture and to interpret meaning behind the words.

There is much current information being written by scientists concerning the great springs that flow into the sea and the great rivers that flow through the sea. In the *Saturday Review* for July 1, 1967 there is an extensive article

31

concerning the many still undetected submarine springs around the world. The statement is made that these fresh submarine springs and rivers are often more common than rivers and surface streams. It is pointed out that in the Persian Gulf there is a major submarine spring with enough volume to create a large area of fresh water in the Indian Ocean! The article tells us that in Greece, a notoriously dry area of the world, an estimated one hundred million cubic feet of fresh water goes into the sea through submarine springs every week. There have been discoveries - most of them since 1960 - of huge rivers in the seas and great "trenches" in the oceans. Several thousand years ago Job asked, "Have you explored the springs of the sea? Or have you walked in the recesses of the deep?" (Job 38:16). Again, if man had made scripture "relevant" how much he would have gained from this passage!

A student of scripture could go on and give reference to "paths of the seas", knowledge of air pressure, stories concerning great construction, how lightning really strikes, etc. These are all there in scripture but *man has chosen to ignore them and instead has substituted dogma.*

One may wonder why I have chosen to write about the "science" facts that are in the Bible in a discourse on making Christianity relevant. I am trying to point out that man has had the tendency to make Christianity non-relevant and not meaningful to many people - especially young people - because *man has used dogmatic creeds and dogmatic ideas to relate Christianity to the modern world and it will not work!*

Our churches often have chosen to ignore those aspects of the teachings which do not conform to some established belief that that particular church had adopted. Man has refused - or at least failed - to bring Christian teachings into sharp focus demonstrating that the basic teachings of Christianity *are* being confirmed and supported by scientific knowledge. Man has not made Christianity *seem* or *appear* practical.

What must man do to really make Christianity relevant and really make God live?

- Man must forget his prejudices, his biases and his dogma. Let him dwell on the Truth of Christianity and forget the ritual and the dogma.

- Man must dwell first and foremost on LOVE. He must start looking for the good in all things - in looking for the good he will find God (Spirit). He must learn to love his neighbors as himself. Many men must learn to love themselves - love themselves in the realization that each is a part of the oneness yet each is unique. *All* are creatures of God. Man must learn that loving one's enemies is the *only* way to overcome. Love is the basic message of Jesus.

- Man must practice the golden rule - if it is practiced no other law - or laws - would ever be needed. What is the real meaning behind the "doing" of the Golden Rule? Man has translated it as *"do* unto others," - the word, "do", implies a thing. If one goes back to the ancient Greek he finds that the word now translated as "do" might just as well be translated as "think" or "thought." I believe it might be important for us to interpret the Golden Rule as "think about others"; then we would not only be doing good to others but thinking good of others which gives us the multiplying power of love. This would make Christianity even more relevant. The idea of thinking unto others as you would have them think unto you removes materialism from the Golden Rule and gives a much broader base for good to come through - both in thought and action.

- One must recognize the scientific fact that ultimately all matter is reduced to energy. Man must see the great relevancy this now established fact has to Christianity. Down through the centuries there have been great debates concerning the nature of matter - indeed, whole philosophies and religions have grown up over this point. When the atom was split it was proven that all matter is reducible to energy. However, since all matter is energy there must be a great storehouse for this energy somewhere and there must be some very effective ways in which to release this energy. All energy has to come from some source! Naturally I have no way of proving this next point one way or another, but could the fact that ultimately all matter becomes energy be the point behind the story found in Genesis concerning man being created in God's image? Perhaps man is being told that God is the source of all energy - that God is energy - and hence man, made up of energy, is created in God's image (pure energy.) Today science has demonstrated the great potential that exists in man through thought - the more positive and loving the thought the more energy that is generated. It has been demonstrated that in dwelling on the past and in dwelling on hatred, one stops growth - and stops generating energy. One finds that in order to generate (release) more energy one must be more loving, one must dwell on the perfection in all things including himself - in other words, one must develop the spirit side of oneself in order to realize the victorious nature of man's Spirit. Spirit will provide the energy if we truly turn to it. If we take any electrical instrument and try to make it regenerate itself from what has already gone through it, it cannot be done! It has to bring in new sources of energy - electricity once expended is gone. Interestingly enough the Bible is full of references to this. The story of Lot and his wife fleeing from Sodom and Gomorrah is a very good example, (An interpretation of the story of Lot is found earlier in this chapter.)

- In making Christianity more relevant man must read and meditate on the scriptures and works of great men with an understanding that they were using the language of their time and attempting to explain *in their environment* great spiritual laws. We need to look at the words metaphysically!

- Perhaps one of the most important of all "forgotten" lessons of Christianity is to look at life with *joy.* We should realize that all of Jesus' teachings were of a very positive nature - Jesus was never negative about anything and His words and acts were full of joy and comfort. Let us not surround Jesus' teachings with too much solemnity and with great ritualistic form - this removes the joy of spontaneity. Medical science (even Freudian psychologists) tell us the importance of enthusiasm, of spontaneous joy, of being of a happy (positive) frame of mind. This was the very heart of Jesus' teaching! We should learn to laugh more, smile at our neighbors, we should start bringing "good cheer" through our words and actions, just as Jesus did. It is through enthusiasm, joy, that our light can shine forth. Joy comes through understanding Truth, truth about our world, about people, ourselves. It comes through an appreciation of ourselves as unique creatures of God. Through having faith in ourselves to relate to others we develop a good personality. A good personality is a "freed" personality - one which does not fear others, which has confidence in its own ability to cope with new situations and "new" people. In Christianity we are taught that all power rests within, that God created each person uniquely, that the Spirit and force of God is with us at all times. We are told so many times in so many ways to have faith and confidence in ourselves - this gives us the "freed", the good personality.

We should have joy in the fact that we are truly free if we want to be - that we are truly protected at all times. In other words, we should have confidence in Jesus' teachings and live by his words and then we will find happiness and understanding and our practice of Christianity will be highly relevant to the world today. We will find the ecstasy and the joy of a *practicing* Christian. We release the victorious Spirit within us and God (Spirit) comes alive for us.

CHAPTER FOUR

Man's Spirit Faculty: The Real "Undernourished" and "Under-developed" Aspect of Modern Man

One of the greatest passages in the Old Testament is Job 32:8, "There is a spirit in man; and the inspiration of the Almighty giveth them understanding." This could be interpreted in several ways, but I choose to believe we are being told that God is prepared to fulfill a need (spiritual development) that He has given us. I believe the implications of this passage are of great importance to us today when the world has turned so much from spiritual things and sought relief, solace and happiness in the material. And the material has completely let us down! Much of the work being done by the behavorial scientists, the psychologists (non-Freudian) in the area of creativity in man now indicates that man must become increasingly aware of nature and the "magic of believing" if he is to be really creative and happily adjusted to life. In *Wings of Healing** by Dean Gresham we find this quote concerning Charles Darwin: "..in one of his letters he tells us out of his own experience how faculties may be lost through disuse. He says that 'Shakespeare whom he once took great delight in, eventually became so intolerably dull to him that even the finest of the plays positively distressed him.' Besides, he lost his taste for music and art, as well as for poetry. He says that 'his mind became a kind of machine for grinding out general laws from large collections of facts'; and that 'this seemed to have atrophied that part of the brain upon which the higher tastes depend.

*The Morgan Company, San Francisco, 1947

"And then he tells us 'that if he had to live his life again he would make it a rule to read some poetry and to listen to some music at least once a week, so that the parts of the brain now atrophied would thus become active through use.

"' The loss of these tastes,' he says 'became a loss to happiness, injurious to the intellect and possibly to the moral nature, because it enfeebled the emotional part of that nature.'"

May not the spiritual faculty, the faculty of and for God, follow the same general law of which Darwin is speaking?

When we look at the words of Elihu's in Job we are given a very clear indication that man has a faculty known as spirituality or spirit. Today modern science calls it intuitive knowledge or the subconscious mind or, in Jung's terms, the collective consciousness. Metaphysicians have always called it the spiritual nature of man. This faculty needs development and nutriment just as the faculties of speech, hearing, seeing, learning, walking, etc. need developing. Who would expect a child to run before he has learned to crawl and walk? Who expects a child to speak before he has heard speech? Who would expect a child to recognize and identify with what he is seeing before he learns what the meaning of the object he is seeing is?

Yet, don't most of us expect that the spiritual faculty shall burst forth"fully grown" without the effort of developing this faculty? Indeed, don't we frequently expect our spiritual aspect - our guide from God - to burst fully upon us at our command?

When Elihu says in Job 32:8, "There is a spirit in man; and the inspiration of the Almighty giveth them understanding", isn't he clearly stating that there is a faculty, called spirit, which can be inspired, developed, through an understanding *and study* of the Almighty?

Through the ages the faculty of spirit has had many names and many interpretations. Sometimes it has been called instinct, sometimes it has been called "creative ability", sometimes it has been known as the Guardian Angel, sometimes we have identified it as extra-sensory perception; and, even more frequently, we have held some sort of fatalistic attitude toward it. When things go wrong we say "it is God's will" (strange how seldom we say it is

37

God's will when things are going well for us! We always seem to put the blame and not the praise on God!)

Probably we have a fatalistic attitude toward tapping the victorious Spirit that is within us because we so seldom nurture it and attempt to develop it. However, would we not also develop a fatalistic attitude toward walking if we did not practice? Would we not develop a fatalistic attitude toward speaking or writing or swimming if we never practiced them?

Perhaps we choose to ignore this faculty because it is the most difficult of all faculties to develop in a thoroughly materialistic and fatalistic society. One does not seek inner strength and understanding to solve material problems until all else has failed! This is so in all materialistic societies. This is the great lesson to be learned from the statement, "count your problems as blessings." This is why the statement, "there are no atheists in the foxhole", is so very true. I know from personal experience how I turned to God twice in my life only through desperation - I didn't learn my lesson the first time. The first experience was during my period as a Naval officer during World War II. As our ship was being shelled by a Japanese battleship and many of our ships were being sunk around us and all seemed lost, everything appeared hopeless. Certainly our protecting fleet was gone, the weather conditions were against us and all logic gained through understanding Naval tactics indicated our situation was hopeless. However, it was then that many of us turned to God, and God answered with what now appears to many to have been a miracle. Knowing the kinds of thoughts with which I was filled and the materialistic emphasis in my life at that time, I doubt if I would have turned to "Spirit" if it had not been for the hopelessness of the situation. Certainly this was a blessing for me even though I did not recognize it as such at the time - I was grateful for having been saved but I gave little credit to God. It took another grave experience in my life to make me keenly aware of the presence of Spirit at all times and of my ability to "release" that presence. How much wiser and happier I would have been years ago if I had just learned to develop my faculty of spirit! It seems that only when all else has failed do we turn inward and search for the kingdom of God which is there - the true spirit faculty.

What we should be doing is to develop this faculty from birth onward just as we develop our ability to speak, walk, comprehend, etc. from infancy. It would be a rare parent, indeed, who did not become concerned if his child was having difficulty in walking, focusing his eyes, detecting sound, etc. Remedial action and additional training and practice would be started immediately. How many parents in our materialistic society become concerned if their child is showing no spiritual understanding? Indeed, many parents and some Freudian psychologists and psychiatrists become quite concerned if the child attempts to use his creative imagination or is an unusually quiet and contemplative youngster!

Anyone who has traveled much, especially in the Oriental and Arab countries, is certain to remark about the happiness and joy he sees in the youngsters - even in the most materially poor areas. A closer investigation would reveal that these youngsters have had lessons, practice and real help in developing the "spiritual faculty." *They have learned how to go "within", how to meditate, how to pray, how to activate the victorious Spirit.* I know many people who say that the typical Oriental of the Buddhist or Hindu persuasion is the most fatalistic of all peoples. This is simply not so. True, the Buddhist and Hindu uses the expression "it is God's will" and they believe in the law of Karma (which is almost the same as the Christian law of sowing and reaping.) However, these groups teach their young that they must do their very best to overcome their handicaps and problems of this lifetime so that they can perfect their bodies, minds and *spirits* so that karma will be fulfilled. They believe that every man has certain obligations to fulfill in this lifetime - but whether or not these obligations are fulfilled is entirely up to the individual. In other words, his spiritual growth is the all important growth. Fatalism does not enter into it in any important way.

One of the greatest of all the lessons that Jesus taught is that we have free will. We are all given certain problems, certain obstacles but how we look at those problems and obstacles, how we handle them, how they affect us, whether they cause us to grow or to stumble is entirely up to us. Our "spiritual faculty development" will determine whether obstacles and problems are our stepping stones and blessings or our graveyards.

The only fatalistic attitude we should hold is that toward our life *if* we don't develop our spiritual faculty. If we leave it unnurtured, untended and undeveloped, then we will have an unfulfilled and unrewarding life *no* matter how materially wealthy we may be. It is the fruits of the spirit that make a man happy, grow, and progress on this Earth plane. It profits a man little to have all the abundance of the world at his command if he does not have inner peace, an inner joy - things of the spirit. We should hearken to the lesson in Mark 10:25, "It is easier for a camel to pass through the eye of a needle than for a rich man to enter the kingdom of God."

Certainly Jesus was not condemning a man simply because he was rich. What he was telling us is that the rich man (rich in health, wealth and other worldly things) has from a material standpoint little reason to turn within - little pressure to seek the world of the Spirit. Hence, he does not develop the faculty of the spirit. He will not be willing to "go within" where lies the "kingdom of God." So many times the man who is poor, who has many problems, who is not fatalistic about all things will be forced to look within and there he finds the kingdom of God.

Fatalism is one of the real "curses" of mankind. If one is completely fatalistic he makes no effort to be creative, he makes no effort to go within, he sees nothing ahead over which he has any control or any motivational ability - he vegetates and does nothing. Of course the greatest problem of the complete fatalist is that he will never make an effort to go within because he sees no reason to go there - what is to be is to be, he seems to say. Yet this is contrary to everything that Jesus taught. Jesus told us in John 14:12-13, "In Truth, in very truth I tell you, he who has faith in me will do what I am doing; and he will do greater things still because I am going to the Father. Indeed anything you ask in my name I will do, so that the Father may be glorified in the Son."

There is certainly nothing fatalistic about that statement of Jesus - one can do anything with the proper development of Spirit! The only thing fatalistic to appear there is perhaps the fatality of *not* developing Spirit! Maybe the majority of the world is right in developing its present fatalistic attitude - it has become a very materialistic and almost "anti-spiritual" world.

The question must be asked, "how does one develop the faculty of spirit?" Just as there is no one best way to develop muscles, reading ability, writing ability, the faculties of observation, hearing, speaking, etc. there is no one best method for developing the faculty of spirit. However, there are certain basics one must understand just as there are certain basics necessary to develop our other faculties even though the techniques vary with the individual and the culture.

I believe the basics that should be kept in mind are:

- periods of quiet - mind and body, Spirit needs to develop without worldly distractions.

- imagination and faith - seeing the beauty in all things and looking for the good in all.

- open mind - attempt to see the visible in the invisible. Know that knowledge in this world is "worldly knowledge" only and not knowledge of the faculty of the Spirit. This knowledge will come from within. As St. Paul said, "the world was created by the word of God so that what is seen was made out of things which do not appear."

- Truth principles - letting go and letting God's ideas come through. This may require inspirational reading, music, etc.

We are taught that there are many roads to God and that each man must find a way to develop the faculty of spirit - each man will have his own way but there will be certain principles in common. If one watches children learning to walk he quickly finds that each child uses a little different technique but all have some basic principles in common. However, *the one great denominator all have in common is the desire to walk and the sure knowledge that walking is possible - a goal! Faith! Patience!*

So, likewise, in developing the spiritual faculty man

41

must have a desire to develop Spirit and the sure knowledge that spiritual development is possible - the goal and faith and patience!

When one develops this faculty of spirit, then he can be *free* of the idea of fatalism - he truly becomes master of his destiny. He frees his creative mechanism to work for him and not against him. He sees his problems as blessings which provide him a stepping stone toward greater spiritual development and show him greater manifestations of the power of Spirit. Above all else he truly feels a part of the kingdom of God. He knows what Jesus meant when He said the kingdom of God is within - he has found and is able to use his victorious Spirit.

We should consider the fact that the Creator provided a "receptacle" for every faculty and capacity provided man: the soul finds expression through forms of beauty, for the heart there is friendship and companionship, for the ear - sound, for the eye - light, for the mind - truth. Would the Creator have provided nothing for the faculty of spirit? Of course not. For this - the faculty of spirit - God Himself was provided. As J. Wilmer Gresham told us in *Wings of Healing**, "...the spiritual faculty, like the physical, the mental, the aesthetic, and all the others, may be developed and cultivated, or neglected and lost."

Probably the greatest summation of what the development of the faculty of spirit can mean to us is provided in Galatians 5:16-25:

"....if you are guided by the Spirit you will not fulfill the desires of your lower nature. That nature sets its desires against the Spirit, while the Spirit fights against it. They are in conflict with one another so that what you will to do you cannot do. But if you are led by the Spirit, you are not under law.

"Anyone can see the kind of behavior that belongs to the lower nature: fornication, impurity, and indecency; idolatry and sorcery; quarrels; a contentious temper, envy, fits of rage, selfish ambitions, dissensions, party intrigues, and jealousies; drinking bouts, orgies, and the like. I warn you, as I warned you before, that those who behave in such ways will never inherit the kingdom of God.

*The Morgan Company, San Francisco, 1947

"But the harvest of the Spirit is love, peace, patience, kindness, goodness, fidelity, gentleness, and self-control. There is no law dealing with such things as these. And those who belong to Christ Jesus have crucified the lower nature with its passions and desires. If the Spirit is the source of our life, let the Spirit also direct our course."

How better could it be said? Paul is telling us that if we develop our spirit faculty we are developing all the worthwhile attributes of man and are truly preparing ourselves for the kingdom of God.

We should begin today to set about on a program to develop the faculty of spirit - just as we set about developing our other faculties when we were in our infancy. We have everything to gain and nothing to lose!

PART TWO

THE ANSWER

Aspects and Manifestations of *Releasing
Man's Victorious Spirit*

Chapters Five through Twelve and
Conclusion

CHAPTER FIVE

The Only Reality

A question that many are asking (or should be asking) is, "How do I relate myself in consciousness to God - to my victorious Spirit?" In order to answer this, one must also ask the question, "What is consciousness?"

Consciousness, according to the dictionaries, is the accumulated knowledge that one has in regard to the world. Of particular importance here are the words *accumulated knowledge.* We accumulate knowledge through experience, education, environment, friends, teachers, and so on. In other words, consciousness is purely a learned reaction or "knowledge" as to what has been given to the individual and the individual's reactions to what has happened - whether a personal experience or an experience of another (history, biography, etc.) Unless an individual has had some spiritual enlightenment, his consciousness normally is composed of purely "worldly" things.

There can be nothing creative about consciousness without the "inner development" of awareness. If we work only with what we know, with what we have seen in our concept of "reality," we make no progress; we stand still. Yet most of us assume that what we hold in consciousness is the only reality. There would have been no great discoveries if men had not been willing to look beyond what their conscious reality said was "real." An Einstein, a Beethoven, a Gandhi, a Michelangelo, a Columbus, a space explorer, had to be willing to assume that his sensory system - his "consciousness" developed through various experiences - was unable to perceive all that is.

We must realize that even our sensory systems (through

which most things enter our consciousness) are activated by learning, by experience. All of us know of blind individuals who have developed almost another "sense" or, at least, have developed their other senses far beyond the norm. They have been forced to give new experiences, "new learning," to their other senses. There are thousands of documented cases in world history of individuals who have more keenly activated senses than is the norm (sometimes feeling, sometimes hearing, sometimes smelling, etc.). As the great British scientist Sir Arthur Eddington put it, "Those who would wish to take cognizance of nothing but the measurements of the scientific world made by our sense-organs are shirking one of the most immediate facts of existence, namely, that consciousness is not wholly, nor even primarily, a device for receiving sense-impressions." Yet for most of us our consciousness consists of what we have allowed the world to put in it, and this consciousness becomes for us all that is real. How limited, how enchained, how lacking in creativity we have allowed our consciousness to make our reality!

Einstein said: "Realization that our knowledge of the universe is simply a residue of impressions clouded by our imperfect senses makes the quest for reality seem hopeless. If nothing has existence save in its being perceived, the world should dissolve into an anarchy of individual perceptions."

Man's ability to be creative comes only through what man puts in his mind - in other words, what he is willing to put into his consciousness. If your reality exists only in terms of what you can see, touch, taste, smell, and hear, then your consciousness has prevented your creative mechanism from functioning at anything like its capacity. What limitations you have set for yourself!

"Ask, and it will be given you; seek, and you will find; knock, and it will be opened to you." This is impossible if one limits his "reality" to his "consciousness." But how very possible this becomes if one recognizes how little *real* perception comes through the consciousness developed only through the sensory system!

Man's Victorious Spirit is not limited by his learned consciousness; it knows that no limitations that have been "learned" are necessarily the final answer. This is the summing-up of the natural law of the relationships between man and his victorious Spirit.

If all men had let only experience dictate to them, the door would have remained closed to new ideas, concepts, creativity. Suppose the first man to discover fire had been burned, and had let that experience (received through the sense of touch) become his complete "consciousness" of fire and had educated all other men on that basis. Would there have been any creative uses of fire? Fortunately, many men realize that one experience, one "lesson," may not be all there is. Certainly we profit by experience, certainly we learn lessons through experience, certainly problems are created and solved through experiences; but experiences (always received in some way through the sensory system) are not all there is.

As Judge Troward said in the "Edinburgh Lectures on Mental Science," "Belief in limitations is the one and only thing that causes limitation, because we thus impress limitation upon the creative principles; and in proportion as we lay that belief aside our boundaries will expand, and increasing life and more abundant blessings will be ours."

We must remember the great basic principle (accepted by psychologists as well as by contemporary theologians) that the only direction, the only thought and power that our consciousness can follow or allow, is what we believe to be reality. We must practice the "magic" of believing. We must feed our consciousness by believing in the actuality of the Spirit, the good, the oneness. We must develop a positive attitude toward what is *not* received via our sensory system; we must have a consciousness of the existence of that which is out of the reach of our sensory system, as strong an awareness as we have of what is within the reach of our senses.

We must recognize that the limitations concerning what we can accomplish, what we can become, what spiritual level we can attain, what we receive from God's abundance, are created by us. If we look for or expect only the things that we have seen, felt, smelt, tasted, or heard, then we are limited to those things. If we have puny expectations concerning ourself and our life, then we will have only puny results.

Those who say they cannot believe in what they cannot consciously recognize through their sensory systems will always be noncreative, stagnant, unrewarded. They have decided to exist in a very small part of the universe, and their growth and development will be limited.

Most of our great scientists (and, of course, all of our great religious teachers) have recognized that consciousness and reality are two very different things. Unfortunately, our consciousness - what we believe concerning our world and our future - is equated by most of us with reality. Actually, reality is what is believed: the consciousness one holds toward all things. If you believe that the physical, material (sensory-received) world is all there is, for you that *is* all there is, or ever will be.

"The world was created by the word of God, so that what is seen was made out of things which do not appear."

When we assume that the only reality is what we know through our sense-organs, we are denying most of what the world today accepts in the whole area of electromagnetism! Have any of us seen the magnetism of the Earth, the causes of gravity, x-rays, how a magnet works, gamma rays, cosmic energy? Certainly not; but we know they exist because some men of unlimited "consciousness" developed machines that recorded the manifestations of these invisible phenomena.

Even in regard to our physical self, we have little ability to know how we function if we rely on our sensory system; we need all sorts of special devices to learn about our cells, our organs, etc. Man has never been able to perceive a virus, either through his sensory system or with special machines. All we see are manifestations of a virus. As Walt Whitman so wonderfully put it, "You are not all included between your hat and your boots."

All of us need to develop a program for "going within" and seeking the kingdom of God - the great victorious Spirit - that is within us. We need to develop an attitude that does not limit us to the puny conceptions we may have of reality. We need to expand our ideas concerning reality beyond what we have placed in our consciousness through experience, education, and environment. Within (and beyond) the visible (conscious) reality of the material body lies the true Spirit - the soul.

We know how the brain functions in the sense of storing information, through the process of a "feed-in." Through our experiences, our lessons, our thoughts, we put information into the "consciousness."

47

However, we also feed this "consciousness" through unconscious reactions to various situations, ideas, experiences. Where the truly creative person varies is in his ability to feed his brain through inner awareness. He is able to tap the visible in the invisible. He is not limited by his sense perceptions.

In the *Metaphysical Bible Dictionary* there is a wonderful interpretation of Matthew 13:33 ("The kingdom of heaven is like yeast, which a woman took and mixed with half a hundred-weight of flour till it was all leavened"): "The leaven is the Truth, and the 'woman' is the soul. When a word of Truth is apparently hidden in the inner mind it is not idle, but quietly spreads until the whole consciousness is light with Spirit. People who have for years had this hidden word of Truth at work in them are quick to respond to a larger exposition of the divine law, and we recognize that they are ripe for receiving Truth." We must place in our consciousness, through prayer and meditation, the yeast (seed), and we will come to recognize that the Truth is the *only* reality. Consciousness, then, will no longer be a limiting factor. We will be free from the chains of limited education, experiences, environment, and can become the creative, joyful, spiritually growing individuals we should be.

CHAPTER SIX

The Teacher of the Way

We all have within us the great master teacher - *the* master teacher - but because we have cloaked the great Spirit within (*the* master teacher) with an illusion of "impossibility" we have failed to recognize that the master teacher is always with us. We fail to understand that the teacher is not outside - not an individual of worldly wisdom - but rather is the great instructor that is within. To be a real student of the greatest of all master teachers requires the dropping of the personality - the ego - and the dropping of worldly concepts and the dropping of preconceived ideas of the nature of wisdom. It requires a recognition that the secret of true success, true happiness and true progress is a consciousness that man has only one reason for life - the return to the great victorious Spirit from which he has been separated. *The* great master teacher that is within each and every man has the answers - the signposts - for the road that returns us to pure Spirit.

But man, ever worldly, unwilling (but not unable) to see the visible in the invisible continues his unrelenting search for *the* teacher outside himself and ever wonders why the teacher has never been found when the search has been so intense, so diligent and so dedicated!

We all know that a man may search forever for a "pearl of great price" but if he searches in places where pearls never develop he obviously will fail. One cannot find anything in a place where nothing is present. A vacuum is a vacuum no matter how one approaches it!

Fortunately for man a few who have lived on this earth have not only been able to find the great master teacher within themselves but have provided some important advice and assistance for those of us who have been unwilling to search in the proper place for our own teacher.

The words found in II Peter 1:3 give us the perfect answer to the reason for the excellence of the great master teacher or master teachers who aid us from the outside. The master teacher gives us through his action his lesson. II Peter 1:3 tells us: "He has by his own action given us everything that is necessary for living the truly good life, in allowing us to know the One Who has called us to virtue and glory."

The master teacher does not convince by words as much as by deeds. Actually the great teacher uses both words and deeds to convey his message.

In planning this message on the master teacher I greatly debated discussing the Socratic, the Aristotelian, the John Dewey, the Montessori ideas of education, I quickly discarded the idea because, in my judgment, the method of teaching is not the important thing. *What is important is the spirit in which the message is both given and received.* It seems to me that this has been too little understood in formal education and, especially, in spiritual teaching.

Perhaps we should remove from our consciousness (at least in teaching spiritual understanding) all concepts of teacher and student. In order for there to be a teacher there must be a student. When there is a student there is elevation (one placed in a higher position than another - one is given authority.) When there is elevation there is judgment (judgment of others is the most destructive of negative forces.) When there is judgment there is separation (separation creates a chasm between individuals and makes exchange of ideas very difficult.) Learning takes place by sharing - it does not take place through judgment and not through separation. If we are to make teaching a very real learning experience for *both* the teacher and the taught, we must make it a sharing experience so that both parties will feel the pertinency and the lack of condemnation - or judgment - within the message.

Jesus, the great master teacher, was very careful to always think, act and relate in terms that were clearly understandable by His "students." He never removed Himself from their surroundings, their world. He understood their language, their history, their religion, their

50

mores, their stories, their parables.

When He talked to the people He was very careful to use the language of the people - He was careful to stay within their vocabulary. He never tried to use words that would give Himself a feeling of superiority and would possibly influence the people to think He was a most learned person even though they would not understand Him.

A really effective teacher knows that learning does not take place by hearing words that are not clearly understood by those who are listening. Jesus recognized the importance of telling stories and parables that were within the common experience of his audience. He knew that in that way He could make the point He was making realistic to his audience. They would understand.

Count Kesselring, one of the world's finest writers in the field of education, often wrote concerning the necessity of teaching within the framework of the existing knowledge of those being taught. He said that learning does not take place - wisdom is not developed - by feeding information alone. Learning - wisdom development - takes place by putting information together with understanding. Students just do not understand if the teacher is speaking from a different frame of reference, is using a different vocabulary. The teacher must do everything possible to develop within himself an understanding - even a love - for the vocabulary, for the stories, for the frames of reference of his students.

Another reason why the terms, teacher and student, are not effective to use in spiritual teaching is that there is the implication that each uses different words in communicating. Again the terms imply elevation of one above the other with the result that there is a tendency of the teacher to start using only his own vocabulary, only his own frame of reference, only his own stories.

The most important prerequisite to be a master teacher is to recognize that a teacher is essentially a student. He must recognize that in his relationship with others he is a sharer and is not in a judgmental position. Once he becomes judgemental he loses his ability to create a real learning experience for those he is teaching.

I am not saying that no discipline is required or maintained. This is an important aspect of the job of the teacher. One maintains discipline primarily through example and never through judgment. The teacher may say you did wrong and correct the action. That is not being judgmental - that is stating a fact about a past experience. However, if the teacher says you did wrong and are a bad boy or you are stupid because you are a mistake-maker that is being judgmental. That not only destroys the teacher-student relationship but also establishes a "seed" in the student's mind of a very negative nature - it may make it nearly impossible for the student to ever again learn in the field in which he was called "stupid". He may now start holding an image of himself as someone without the ability to learn in that area.

The teacher must be very careful never to condemn - condemnation utterly destroys the condemned's ability to learn, the ability to progress, the ability to think positive in that area. It also places a great feeling of guilt and feeling of dislike on the shoulders of the individual who condemned. Until the condemner asks to be forgiven for his action of condemnation he will carry this guilt and this feeling of hate (or great disliking) with him and that is most self-destructive.

Jesus never condemned, never judged, those who rejected His teachings, even persecuted him because of His teachings. He did not have to forgive because He never condemned. In the story of the adulterous woman Jesus did not forgive her, He simply said, "go forth and sin no more." He did not call her a sinner, He did not fix in her mind the idea that she was an adulterer. Hence, she was freed from the necessity of overcoming a bad image of herself - she was now "clean" and ready to start a new, better life. Jesus did not forgive her because He had never condemned her. This was acting as a "master teacher".

From what I can learn through studying early Roman Catholicism and the development of Church rules and dogma, it appears to me that the major reason for the confession was to make man free of the idea that he is a sinner - that he is outside God's grace and God's understanding. The idea behind the confession is that man is not condemned for what he did - he does not have to be forgiven because he has not been condemned. He can leave the confessional feeling that he is not a sinner; but rather now he has paid for his transgression. It is over and forgotten about and he is not to be thought of as the wicked individual who performed that wicked act. In his consciousness he can now feel free to start fresh in life and not think of himself as a wicked person from whom society and God expect nothing except wickedness. If this was the original idea of the confession, it was a very sound one. Certainly modern psychology has learned that man conforms to the image he has of himself. If he thinks of himself as a sinner, he will conform to that image. If he now thinks of himself as free of sin, then the image he can hold of himself can be a most constructive one and be free of negativity. We can profit much from understanding this principle in regard to our children with learning problems, with former criminals who have paid their debt to society, etc. If a child thinks of himself as "backward" or "retarded" then he will conform to that image and it will be practically impossible for him to become anything but retarded or backward. If the former prison inmate is released from prison but is truly not forgiven, is kept reminded that he is a felon, is kept informed that he is a criminal, then the image he has of himself will be that of an individual outside society; and he will conform to that image.

A good teacher knows he should never use the expression, "You are forgiven this time but I am not forgetting what you did." That is anything but forgiving and the individual involved will constantly be aware that you are remembering that he was bad and he may very well conform to that image. How many parents have said, "I forgive but I am not forgetting?" We must start practicing not only forgiving but also forgetting!

Another benefit of the confession was that no score - or record - was kept of the number of sins for which an individual had been forgiven. Hence, he could always start with a fresh, healthy image.

I know how the confession has often been distorted - some even saying, "Oh, well, I can always be forgiven when I confess." (The Church does have very special ways of handling those who think in this manner.) Of course, any great principle can be abused and the principle behind the confession is no exception.

One may wonder if I have not wandered a great deal from my topic, The Master Teacher. I don't believe I have at all because what I am trying to do is indicate that it is in sharing in life, in expressing love, in learning lessons together, that the real teaching takes place. The real learning goes on in the classroom of life not in the formal classroom - at least the real learning in terms of helping man find his way to the victorious Spirit within him.

Jesus, as Mohammed and Buddha, did most of his teaching through talking to groups at various places, by examples he made, by demonstrating what He meant by love, what were the results of condemnation and forgiveness. He never wrote a book, He gave only one major sermon (The Sermon on the Mount) and that was not done through formal preparation. He became the great master teacher by *sharing* His experiences, His knowledge, His intuition, His instinct, and especially His love.

The men who have made a mark in this world in elevating man's consciousness have done it through a sharing process - not through the very formal teacher-student relationship with all its elevation, judgment, and separation!

The master teacher realizes he must provide incentive, motivation, a goal. In I Corinthians 14:8 Paul says: "For if the trumpet give an uncertain sound, who shall prepare himself to the battle?"

I believe it is the job of the teacher to give a loud and clear call (motivation) through action as well as through speaking. Jesus never asked us to do anything that He was not willing to do and to do with love and understanding. Any teacher should so believe in what he is teaching that he can give a loud and clear call to his students. This is so especially true in the spiritual field where we are all teachers and we are all students. We must believe, thoroughly believe, in what we are doing and we must not be afraid to set an example and speak out. We should be truly willing to let all know - and see - the spiritual world in which we live. How can we play our role as teacher with effectiveness if our faith does not shine forth? Our students must be able to hear the trumpet loud and clear.

Many of us with experience in the business world and particularly in the sales field are quite conscious of the disaster that will overtake the salesman who does not believe in what he is selling or has lack of faith in himself. If he lacks confidence in either the product or himself, clients quickly become aware of this lack of conviction and refuse to respond to the sales message.

The master teacher recognizes the fact that any lack of firmness in his resolve, lack of understanding of his goals, lack of faith in his relationship to Spirit, would make him ineffective in teaching others.

The student is taught by example and by action more than he is taught by words. If you think back through your life what were the great learning experiences for you? Unless you are most unusual they occurred when you saw something demonstrated or actually had an experience yourself - something within your frame of reference to which you could relate. You did not learn to read by looking at words - you learned to read by listening to others read, looking at the words as they did so and by trying to read yourself; you learned mathematics in very much the same manner.

As students trying to find our way back to man's victorious Spirit we have to practice - seeing examples of people who have done it helps, parables of how and why it is done are very helpful - but above all else we must practice. The job of the teacher is to encourage us, to give us faith, to set an example, to demonstrate. These things are all done by sharing - not by threatening, not by condemning, not by lecturing per se, etc.

We so often need encouragement both as teachers and students. Several little expressions which I find helpful are these:

"Knowledge is not a thing of writ,
An education, nor the lack of it -
'Tis simply the balancing
Of a temporal hour
With the fragile melody of a flower."
(author unknown)

The world is made of signs - but only when man is seeking direction are they meaningful.

Only in Spirit does one man understand another.

There is an old Hindu expression I greatly admire: When the pupil is ready the teacher appeareth.

I feel certain that what is meant by this last expression

is that when the motivation is strong enough, when the desire to learn is great, the means for learning will be provided. The other expressions I just gave have almost the same meaning.

The master teachers who were interested in helping man find his way to God (the victorious Spirit) knew that strong motivation had to exist within a man before he would be willing to truly seek the path to spiritual enlightenment.

Many Eastern religions teach that it is necessary to suffer greatly before one truly seeks to learn (or can learn) the way to God. In other words, they seem to say that it is through suffering that man gains the incentive to study and learn practical truths.

I believe this attitude is quite different than the attitude held by Jesus and by Buddha. Although both Jesus and Buddha recognized that man had to be greatly motivated before he would become a very real student of the spiritual path, this motivation did not have to come through suffering. Certainly Jesus emphasized that in believing His word, in following His action one could avoid much of the suffering of the world.

However, it certainly is true that in our world with the great emphasis on materialism most will not turn and become students of spiritual truths and find their own master teacher until their backs are against the wall - until all the material world has let them down and failed them. I suppose this is why we should often count our problems as our blessings - when we have problems which cannot be answered by the material things and ideas of the world, we are forced to look "within". We are forced to become students - we now have the motivation to learn, to observe, to demonstrate the power of spiritual understanding.

With the desire for spiritual enlightenment, *the pupil is ready!* The teacher always appears when man gives up seeking all answers within the material world because the victorious Spirit of man is always available - it is just waiting the readiness of the pupil to receive!

One can see that, once again, learning is a sharing - both the pupil and the teacher must be ready (both must be motivated) and one cannot give the initial motivation to the other. The pupil must develop an awareness of a need and the teacher must be ready with the answer for that need. Fortunately, the teacher, that is the victorious Spirit in man, is always available whenever the pupil is ready. It becomes a sharing of what each has.

Finally in discussing the master teacher it should be clearly stated that the teacher, if he is truly to be a "master" teacher, must know the true meaning of love - especially the aspect of love that desires the total fulfillment of the abilities within man. A master teacher, such as Jesus, desires each student to develop his own uniqueness - to free his own creativity. The creative aspect of man is the material aspect closest to God.

One does not have to be a poet, a painter, a composer, a writer to be creative - all men can be creative in some area. It may be in inventions, in concepts, in management, in doing the most menial of jobs. There is no activity of man in which creativity cannot be demonstrated. It is the teacher's role to assist the student in releasing his creative element. The ability to stand in wonder of a great sunset, of a great tree, or of a small stone, or flower, or insect - are all things to be encouraged by the teacher because all lead the observer to see the "invisible in the visible" - which makes for a giant step toward creativity.

Creativity is the taking of the ordinary - or the known - and making something different from it (this can be an idea as well as a thing.) The challenge to the master teacher is to provide the "spark" that starts the pupil looking for the "invisible in the visible."

There are many challenges for the master teacher but there are just as many for the student. Both must recognize that they are in a sharing relationship and neither gains unless both are willing to share in their love and understanding. The master teacher can help to light the way for the student but he cannot make him walk the way. The student must be willing to make the effort to walk on the path to knowledge. No man can walk forward and backward at the same time so the goal must be firmly established so that there will be forward progress.

The teacher must remember and be encouraged by the fact that as a guide marks the trail he also reaches the goal!

The great art of the master teacher is the art of creating an awareness of the beauty, the hope, the glory that exists within man's victorious Spirit. How beautifully Jesus, the greatest of the master teachers, performed this art! And how great the fact that each of us has within himself "a master teacher" ready to aid him in his journey back to pure Spirit - the victory within!

CHAPTER SEVEN

Non-Resistance: The Law

I doubt if anything in theology has been more misunderstood, more misinterpreted, nor more mis-represented than Jesus' admonition in His Sermon on the Mount that man must "resist not evil." This is one of the most important messages that Jesus brought to us and it was one of the sharpest departures He made from the orthodox Hebrew teachings.

I like the New English Bible's translation of the section concerning resistance to evil in the Sermon on the Mount. It is found in Matthew 5:38-48: "You have learned that they were told, 'An eye for an eye, and a tooth for a tooth.' But what I tell you is this: Do not set yourself against the man who wrongs you (resist not evil.) If someone slaps you on the right cheek, turn and offer your left. If a man wants to sue you for your shirt, let him have your coat as well. If a man in authority makes you go one mile, go with him two. Give when you are asked to give; and do not turn your back on a man who wants to borrow.

"You have learned that they were told, 'Love your neighbor, hate your enemy.' But what I tell you is this: Love your enemies and pray for your persecutors; only so can you be children of your heavenly Father, who makes his sun rise on good and bad alike, and sends the rain on the honest and the dishonest. If you love only those who love you, what reward can you expect? Surely the tax gatherers do as much as that. And if you greet only your brothers, what is there extraordinary about that? Even the heathen do as much. You must therefore be all goodness, just as your heavenly Father is all good."

What a marvelous lesson in Truth! - whether it is Truth from a Christian theology sense, whether from a psychological sense, or from a practical sense! We know from all types of psychological studies that when we dwell on anything it becomes dominant in our mind - all our creative energy, all our knowledge, all our awareness focuses in on what we are dwelling on. Hence, if we resist anything the very action of resisting gives substance to what we are resisting. We give it strength to move us - *not* we it! The only reality in our world is what we recognize! If we resist anything we give it reality.

So many misunderstand the law of *non*resistance - the "resist not evil" of which Jesus spoke. So many believe it is the coward's way, the way of those who are not capable of defending themselves, the way of those who feel weak themselves and in faith in regard to their goals or objectives.

How far from the truth is the belief that non-resistance is the weakling's way! The individual who practices non-resistance is far stronger than the one who practices resistance. To be nonresistant to anything requires great courage both of body and mind. Above all else non-resistance requires great activation of the victorious Spirit within, and it requires the true practice of love. *Non-resistance is the triumph of the mind over the body and the spirit over the mind.*

The man who has little mind control over the body lashes out at whatever is "evil" in his world, he exerts his physical energy to hit at the "evil" and he gains no lasting dominion over that evil. The man who has little spiritual control of his mind works through worldly knowledge scheming and planning on how to outwit, outmaneuver and gain advantage over "evil". In both cases, there is great resistance to evil - either of body or mind. But the man who has gained spiritual enlightenment - who understands Jesus' message - neither physically or mentally exerts his energy to strike out against the "evil" he finds in the temporal affairs of himself and others. He keeps his body, mind and spirit on what is eternal - man's need to return to complete spiritual understanding, Christ Consciousness. As Jesus told us in a passage in The Sermon on the Mount, "Love your enemies and pray for your persecutors." This is the way to the victorious Spirit that is within. Naturally to love one's enemies requires great courage, great faith, great intestinal fortitude - it is the most courageous of all action that could be taken and it demonstrates true spiritual understanding.

We must not confuse nonresistance with taking the "line of least resistance." They are far different. Taking the "line of least resistance" is still resisting - it still is contrary to the admonition of "resist not evil." The line of least resistance is often the coward's way out and is certainly an evasion of personal responsibility. Nonresistance requires that we meet the problem or the situation head-on; but that we meet it with love, in serenity and with peace in the sure knowledge that if we are following Truth all is well and that there is good in the adversity that is present. After all, God created all and is in all and through all. Nonresistance does not mean we surrender - it means that we recognize that our primary goal in life is "returning to pure spirit," and we accept our responsibilities along the way to that goal. Nonresistance never means we ignore our responsibilities - on the contrary, it means we accept our responsibilities with love realizing that they will help us to grow in consciousness and in spirit. Nonresistance simply means that our attitude toward our responsibilities and toward the adversities and enemies that challenge us in life is one of acceptance and love. *Resistance* to our responsibilities, to our adversities, to our enemies means that we do *not* accept the fact that God created all and that God is providing us with a way of attaining a higher degree of spiritual enlightenment.

One should consider the many ways in which most of us practice resistance. We do it through judging ourselves and others, through opposition, through resentment, through gossip, through jealousy and above all through disliking and hating. Most of us do not resist primarily through physical action although that is a pattern that some follow. In the act of resisting we are manifesting the fact that the temporal has dominion over us - that our spiritual consciousness has not risen to the point where it has much dominion over us. Resistance demonstrates that the personality is still blocking us from an awareness of spiritual truth. It shows that we are still more concerned with our personality (the world self) than we are with the most important aspect of ourselves which is our spiritual development. To truly practice nonresistance one must drop the personality (the worldly aspects of self) in favor of the spiritual self.

Only the greatest of evolved beings on this earth have been able to practice complete nonresistance. Most of us dwell on the words of our enemies, the acts of our enemies, the objectives and motives of our enemies because they mitigate or tend to crush or cloud our worldly image of ourselves - in some manner or means they create a lesser image of ourselves. It is a psychological fact, widely recognized in education, that man does not learn effectively - often does not comprehend - until he feels personally involved (his personality is involved.) Hence, we really get excited - we really "resist" - when we find our personality attacked. However, once we are aware of the temporal nature of "personality" - that it is only important in the worldly sense - then we begin on the path to spiritual enlightenment and we can begin to practice true nonresistance.

We must not confuse nonresistance and resistance to temptation. When we are practicing nonresistance we do not resist with body, mind or spirit an *existing* situation, problem or idea. Toward *all that exists* we hold the attitude of love, tolerance and understanding. Temptation is something that *could* occur, something that is before us but does not yet exist for us as a condition, a problem or a situation. Resisting temptation means simply dismissing the possibility of succumbing to a condition that could occur. This is not at all the same thing as Jesus was talking about when He admonished us to "resist not evil". Temptation has to do with a "potential" condition and we avoid it through keeping our mind on our true objective, on the reason for our existence. In a sense we don't resist temptation, we simply dismiss it knowing that to succumb to it would place a block on our path to spiritual understanding. Really all temptation ever is is an attempt by the body or mind to divert our spiritual side from having dominion over the trinity of body, mind and spirit. Temptation represents the temporal side of man attempting to seduce the "entire" man. It is not truly resisted - it is simply dismissed as an unnecessary detour on our pathway to enlightenment.

When we think of examples of men who have practiced

nonresistance, most of us think of Gandhi. Of course, he probably more greatly manifested the law of nonresistance than anyone else in the last two centuries. Gandhi certainly changed the world and most of the peoples of the world through his practice of true nonresistance. He did not lash back when his personality was attacked, he did not hate his enemies (just the opposite), he did not physically resist when physical attacks were made. He just maintained a calm, quiet assurance in the truth and the justice of what he believed. He was firm in his faith and in his conviction; and he demonstrated his great faith with love and did so with every situation which he met - he even created opportunities to demonstrate his love. Certainly, it was through his perseverence with nonresistance that he won the great victory. He even won the admiration and respect of his enemies. Lincoln, too, was a great believer in nonresistance. One only has to read a few of his addresses to be very aware of this - he spoke of the firm conviction that right would triumph, of the necessity for mercy and understanding for those who were opposed to his objectives, of the need to get on with the job of rebuilding and not become immersed in rivalries, jealousies, revenge and resentment.

It is important to read and study the entire Sermon on the Mount to truly comprehend Jesus' great admonition to "resist not evil". He tells us in various ways that nonresistance accepts generalizations and is not bogged down in details, that our mind must be acceptable to agreements (not compromise but agreement), that nonresistance requires a recognition that God is in all, through all, with all; and therefore there are no superiorities or inferiorities among people. Jesus asks us to recognize not the differences in people but the similarity - a very basic requirement in learning to love. He tells us that one must recognize that God created all; and since that is true, then there is basic good in all and we must search out the good and focus on it.

Another basic truth which becomes self-evident when one studies the nature of the admonition "love your enemies" is the fact that *if you don't consider yourself an enemy you have no enemies.* You create enemies by attitudes you hold toward others. If you look upon others with love and understanding, they will not be enemies.

Only we, ourselves, can create enemies for ourselves by believing - giving substance to, resisting - what we consider to be threats to our personalities. If we dwell on the good in others, we quickly will discover that there is something to like within all beings and all things. It is going to be very difficult to imagine an enemy as anyone within whom one has found something to like! The lessons of "resist not evil" and "love your enemies" certainly belong together and they are found together in the Sermon on the Mount - Matthew 5:39 (resist not evil) and Matthew 5:44 (love your enemy.) You simply have no enemies if you practice love; and if you practice real love, you practice nonresistance - you resist not evil.

We must learn not to resist the opinions others hold toward us. Their opinions are no concern of ours. If we become concerned it shows that we are still allowing our personality to dominate us. If we are truly seeking the road which will reunite us with Spirit then the opinions held by others are of no concern. When we are on the right path many will criticize; but we must remember they are criticizing from ignorance or from an awareness that you have something they don't have - they are jealous. Then, too, they are viewing you from worldly attitudes and from worldly perceptions. Let your light so shine forth that they can learn how they, too, can walk on a spiritual path to return home again. But don't let your personality, which may be trying to resist the evil said about you, stand in the way of your spiritual progress. Try more and more to ignore - nonresist - the demands of the personality and surely the sting of malicious words said by others about you will lose their bite. If you can conduct yourself without resistance and in harmony when an injustice is done you, you are truly on the road to personal peace, harmony and spiritual enlightenment. You must remember that only by resisting through holding an attitude of resistance can a real injustice, real harm, real destruction be done you by others!

Psychologically it is a fact that most people lose their peace of mind, lose their self-respect, even can become paranoid through allowing criticism by others - especially malicious and untrue criticism - to become important to them. They are resisting the evil! Jesus was the great psychologist - nothing in His words is contrary to anything currently known by psychologists; and His word is still far beyond the most advanced of our psychological studies. Nothing is stressed more in psychology today than the problems that come to an individual through his dwelling on criticism - either by others or by self. This criticism is directed at personality; and Jesus has told us so many times to both drop the personality (the worldly self) in favor of the spiritual development of self and to "resist not evil" - ignore the barbs of others. Certainly, Jesus, the great teacher, the great healer, the great psychologist, has given us many powerful messages on the importance of dwelling on the good, of looking within, of seeking spiritual understanding. These are very positive things. He gave us lessons in nonresistance long before it became a popular idea among mankind.

Much of the criticism made by the orthodox Hebrew church of Jesus' time was levied at Jesus because of His admonition to "resist not evil". Many felt that this was not an effective way of handling the tax collector, the foreign armies of Rome, the dictatorship imposed by Rome. They did not follow Jesus' admonition - just as we do not today - and there was and has been no peace in the world. Look what Gandhi accomplished through practicing Jesus' way! Look at what the Hebrews did *not* accomplish by their practice of resistance!

I know that to many the whole idea of nonresistance seems very esoteric, very unrealistic, very impractical. I would ask that those who feel this way about nonresistance ask themselves what has been accomplished by resisting evil - whatever they may consider "evil" to be. Has resistance ever made for peace? Has resistance ever stamped out an evil? Has resistance to malicious gossip or unfair accusations ever corrected the situation or led to the truth? Don't many still say "where there is smoke there must be fire?" In a few isolated and minor cases one many find an example of resistance aiding the situation. But almost without exception resistance has led to no resolution of the problem, has led to no real understanding, has led to the opening of more wounds and more hatred. It is through example that we effectively overcome the barbs, the wicked acts, the animosities of others (our enemies.) It is through having a steadfast purpose, through having great faith in the goodness in ourselves and others, through seeking the victorious Spirit that is within ourselves that we truly conquer our enemies. In other words, the real accomplishments in terms of overcoming our enemies are made when we are nonresistant. When we actively resist, we are giving strength to the very thing we are resisting because we give substance and energy to it. When we resist - which means we must dislike whatever we are resisting - we give great attention to what we resist. This gives it great power and dominion over us because our minds are now consciously focused on it, and we are not able to be about our "Father's business". It becomes *the* focal point of our existence at the time we are resisting. We know in modern psychology that in order to break a bad habit one must not focus on that habit - one must find something else to think about, one often must find a substitution. When we make this substitution automatically it is called sublimation. When we have a habit we are trying to break, authorities recognize that calling attention to the habit will only aggravate it and make us more conscious of the need to continue in the old way. Psychologists tell us habits can only be broken by taking the attention elsewhere. When we resist anything we focus on it; and therefore, we become enslaved by it just as we become enslaved by habits. Certainly, then, if we wish to overcome evil in our world we are not going to do so if we actively resist it. We must focus on the good that is within us and all things and keep our focus on the good - that is nonresistance. In some cases, nonresistance could be called a form of sublimation.

"Resist not evil" is not an unrealistic approach to "evil" at all. It does not mean we ignore the situation and that we don't try to do the best we can to improve the world. It is simply that we don't resist it - we flow with it in terms of what is good in it and ignore the rest.

Have you ever observed a leaf floating down a stream and noted how beautifully it flows when the deep pool and the calm waters seem to be its destination? The leaf, if it had intelligence, might find rocks or twigs that are in the stream and see them as an evil (something that will stop the leaf from reaching its destination) - but how often the leaf would be torn and broken by detouring itself from its destination at the calm pool by attacking the rocks and twigs, things it saw as evil. Isn't man often very much as the leaf? He so often overlooks the objective of life - the great calmness of the spiritual "pool" - and is detoured by the evils he sees around him and he loses his great goal by resisting (attacking) the current evil. Just as the leaf he is often crushed while in the very place he thought he could destroy evil by resisting.

We so often lose our sense of direction - our goal - by being too concerned with what evil there is around us. If we keep our eye on our goal in life, if we "turn the other cheek" to evil said about and done to us, then our enemies cannot hurt us. If we can come into spiritual enlightenment nothing else is of any importance. We can only come into this enlightenment if we practice nonresistance to the trials, tribulations, criticisms, animosities, jealousies and hatreds of this world - if we focus on the goodness and the perfection of God's world.

Nonresistance is the most practical of activities in which we can engage - and nonresistance is an activity. It does require action - the action of seeking good and creating good in what is around us. It is just as practical in business, in law, in medicine, in work of any kind as anything that could be named. It is *not* an impractical philosophy. Man must recognize that resistance can only create more hatred, more evil, more strife and destroy creative ability. True, active, nonresistance can work because it can change not just our current activities and consciousness but consciousness and events for eternity.

Nonresistance is the *law* that must be observed and lived by if one is to release the great victorious Spirit that is within. As with any law, its great value and its great service can be observed only by abiding by it. The law of nonresistance is a necessity for all those who wish to walk in safety, assurance and love on their pathway to Spirit (God.)

CHAPTER EIGHT

Love: The Key

Nothing is more basic to Christianity than Love - nothing is more emphasized, more discussed, more eulogized, more urged, more enthusiastically endorsed. Yet with modern man nothing in all of our religion or of our basic belief is more misunderstood, misinterpreted or *ignored*.

What has happened to have caused man, to whom love was given and upon whom love was urged, to so misunderstand and to so ignore love?

In my opinion what has happened is that man has chosen to leave Spirit out of Love and to consider love from purely a materialistic - a sensory - standpoint. As with so many aspects of life man has refused to accept what is not material to him. He refuses to believe in those things and concepts which he cannot see in a physical sense. For most men today nothing exists except that which is visible in some way to the sensory system - that which man can feel, taste, smell, see or hear.

Hence, love for modern man is basically thought of in a sexual sense (feel). When one says "love" today the Freudian and Hollywood concept comes immediately to mind - man seems to say "if it is love it has to do with sex and sexual relationships." Many individuals are very much afraid of expressing love even in speech and feel great pangs of guilt because they feel love for someone or something. These guilt "pangs" often exist even when one just feels great kinship with another and so he never openly expresses this wonderful, brotherly feeling.

What has happened, of course, is that man has taken

Jesus' meaning of love and distorted it through making it a purely material thing. Everything one reads in scripture would lead one to understand that *love was meant to be an attitude* - an attitude of understanding, an attitude of non-condemnation, an attitude of appreciation. Love was a manifestation of man's victorious Spirit. Love was the manner by which man could come into harmony with his fellow man, with his environment, with his true self. Love was the avenue to true Spirit - it was the way to God. God is love, God is good - when love is manifest in an individual he is truly God-like, he truly is in communion with Spirit.

When one truly has love he radiates a light and a joy that manifests itself by being reflected back, in and through others. Isn't this what Jesus did? Wasn't Jesus constantly telling us that love leads to God because God is love?

I believe it is time that man began to reappraise and re-assess what love really means. Before the Seventeenth Century in Biblical translations the word, "charity", often appears where modern translations use the word, "love". The word was changed from "charity" to "love" because of the change that had come into the meaning of "charity". At one time "charity" meant a sharing, an understanding, an appreciation, a brotherliness. Even today in Webster's one finds that the first and preferred definition of "charity" is love! Maybe, because of Twentieth Century distortions in the use of the word, "love", we need a new word to describe what Jesus - and practically every great religious teacher of all faiths - meant by love!

Somehow love has become attached to sexual activity - and often sexual activity which is completely devoid of anything other than animalistic desire. One cannot blame the Freudians entirely for this - although the Freudian emphasis on the sexual drive in man certainly has had a role to play.

I noted in the press reporting of a very sordid trial that a witness testified that she had made love a number of times with a defendant and others. Obviously she was referring to the sex act - an act probably pretty much devoid of love in the true sense. The thing that was rather startling is that the press picked this up as an apt description of the sexual act - "we made love".

I think it is time that society began to realize that the sexual act may be a manifestation of great attraction and

69

great love but it is not love in itself. Love certainly can exist, and usually does exist, without sexual activity. Sexual activity unfortunately can and often does exist without any love whatsoever. The two are certainly in no way synonomous!

I again go back to the idea that perhaps we are misunderstanding what Jesus meant by love through semantic problems and maybe we should seek a new term just as at one time we changed from the word, "charity", to the word, "love". If one looks up the word, "love" in Webster's he finds the following: "affection based on admiration or benevolence; an assurance of love; warm attachment; enthusiasm or devotion; the object of such attachment or devotion; unselfish concern that freely accepts another in loyalty and seeks his good; the attraction based on sexual desire; a beloved person; a score of zero in tennis; when in capitals Christian Science uses it as GOD." Note how far down in preferred meanings Webster places the sexual aspect of love. Yet, most of modern man would place the sexual aspect as number one.

I have dwelt long enough on the semantic problems we have with the word, "love". I have dwelt upon this point at some length because I believe the sexual concept of love has caused many people to feel very uncomfortable in thinking about or discussing "love". Because the word has a certain degree of uncertainty (at least in the minds of most) about it - the idea of love - they choose to ignore it. We always avoid dwelling on those things which cause us to feel insecure.

As a result most of modern man is missing the most rewarding experience possible and he is missing the only direct road to God - the direct road (the key) to the great victorious Spirit of man is through understanding, appreciating and manifesting love.

If one wants to find an apt description of love and an excellent model to follow in learning the art of loving, he has only to turn to I Corinthians, Chapter 13 and 14:1 -

"I may speak in tongues of men or of angels, but if I am without love, I am a sounding gong or a clanging cymbal. I may have the gift of prophecy, and know every hidden truth; I may have faith strong enough to move mountains; but if I have no love, I am nothing. I may dole out all I possess, or even give my body to be burned, but if I have no love, I am none the better.

"Love is patient; love is kind and envies no one. Love is never boastful, nor conceited, nor rude; never selfish, not quick to take offense. Love keeps no score of wrongs; does not gloat over other men's sins, but delights in the truth. There is nothing love cannot face; there is no limit to its faith, its hope and its assurance.

"Love will never come to an end. Are there prophets? their work will be over. Are there tongues of ecstasy? they will cease. Is there knowledge? it will vanish away; for our knowledge and our prophecy alike are partial, and the partial vanishes when wholeness comes. When I was a child, my speech, my outlook, and my thoughts were all childish. When I grew up, I had finished with childish things. Now we see only puzzling reflections in a mirror, but then we shall see face to face. My knowledge now is partial; then it will be whole, like God's knowledge of me. In a word, there are three things that last forever; faith, hope, and love; but the greatest of them all is love.

"Put love first."

Paul gives us many lessons in the real meaning of love besides that found in I Corinthians 13 - I believe some passages in Romans are very important in understanding love.

Romans 13:7-10: "Discharge your obligations to all men; pay tax and toll, with reverence and respect, to those to whom they are due. Leave no claim outstanding against you, *except that of mutual love.* He who loves his neighbor has satisifed every claim of the law. For the commandments 'Thou shalt not commit adultery, thou shalt not kill, thou shalt not steal, thou shalt not covet', and any other commandments there may be, are all summed up in the one rule, 'Love your neighbor as yourself.' Love cannot wrong a neighbor; therefore, the whole law is summed up in love."

Romans 14:1-4: "If a man is weak in his faith you must accept him without attempting to settle doubtful points. For instance, one man will have faith enough to eat all kinds of food, while a weaker man eats only vegetables. The man who eats must not hold in contempt the man who does not, and he who does not eat must not pass judgment on the one who does; for God has accepted him."

Romans 14:13-18: "Let us therefore cease judging one another, but rather make this simple judgment: that no obstacle or stumbling block be placed in a brother's way. I am absolutely convinced, as a Christian, that nothing is impure in itself; only, if a man considers a particular thing impure, then to him it is impure. If your brother is outraged by what you eat, then your conduct is no longer guided by love. Do not by your eating bring disaster to a man for whom Christ died! What for you is a good thing must not become an occasion for slanderous talk; for the kingdom of God is not eating and drinking, but justice, peace, and joy inspired by the Holy Spirit. He who thus shows himself a servant of Christ is acceptable to God and approved by men."

I have quoted from scripture at some length because I think it is very important for all to understand what Biblical authors have felt was the true meaning of love - how *it is the very basis of all the teachings!*

In reading or hearing what has been said about love - and I have just barely touched on what is in the Bible in this respect - it becomes very obvious that love is an understanding, a respect for all life (all creation), an attempt to look for the good in all things and peoples, an attempt not to look back but to look ahead and at the present, an absence of condemnation, an absence of negative judgment, an absence of negative appraisal of our environment and our circumstances. One should note how one must learn to look at all things in a favorable light; e.g.: we are admonished to pay our taxes and tolls to the collectors with reverence and respect, we are not to judge those whose desires in food are different than our own, we are not to look at things or ideas with the idea that they are impure (Paul said: "I am absolutely convinced, as a Christian, that nothing is impure in itself; only, if a man considers a particular thing impure, then to him it is impure.")

To me, at least the basic idea behind love is to treat all creatures and all things with respect - to attempt to see the good in all. Many years ago America's great philosopher, Emerson, said that mental health is the propensity to look for good in all. How right he was!

How important throughout the message on love is the *admonition not to judge.* When we are judging we are denying the God in others. We are proclaiming somebody as being less than God-like. We are denying God's presence in all, through all, with all.

If we are to truly manifest love with meaning for ourselves and for others we must recognize that when we condemn either ourselves or others we are denying the perfection of God. We are denying the victorious Spirit in man. Certainly we can with love say that what was done was wrong or we or someone did wrong, but we must not say he is bad or I am weak or I am bad. When we do that - proclaim ourselves or others as weak, bad or non-God-like - we are expressing the very antithesis of love. *We are declaring in our condemnation that God is not perfect. Since God is love and our road to God is through love, when we condemn we destroy the bridge to others and to God.*

I believe that the true meaning of love is the propensity - the ability if you wish - to see good in all. That is, to see the God (the perfection) in all. It is the ability to overlook the weaknesses that are present in ourselves and others, to see the strengths and the potential strengths. It is the ability not to condemn for past errors, hurts and slanders given us by others (of course if we never condemn we never have to forgive.) It is the ability to look for the God perfection in ourselves and others. It is the willingness to see that the gifts we have are gifts from God and therefore we are not boastful. It is the humbleness we can feel through the knowledge that we still have a way to go to perfect the God-force (the great victorious Spirit) within us. It is *not* a humbleness that we are lesser men than other men because our love tells us that we are all God's creatures. Above all else love is the ability to feel in

73

harmony with all life and to look for the good in all.

When man begins to really comprehend the great lessons of what "love" really is, then he can start to realize the great multiplying power of love. Love is probably the only thing in the world which multiplies by division!!! The more love I can manifest and give out the more love I attract. The more love I attract the more I can give out.

It is my belief that the admonition found in the scriptures of the disciples (Matthew 24:14, Mark 13:10; Luke 24:47) to go forth and preach the words of Jesus to all the nations had very specific reference to the multiplying power of love.

If the missionaries of the fourteenth century until the present had preached in terms of love and in terms of the positives and had not been so concerned about making natives conform to dogma and foreign environments what a different world this would have been. And how more rapidly true Christianity would have spread! However, the missionaries attempted to spread their word through dogma - rarely did they even consider looking for good (love) among the natives - with the result that mankind and Christianity were given a severe blow.

Contrast the missionaries of the past few centuries with an Albert Schweitzer or a Tom Dooley! How wonderful the "spreading of the word" can be if one uses as the basis of the "word" the concept of love - looking for the good!

The multiplying power of love is such a powerful thing that man has probably been a little afraid to place it in full use - that is, if man has ever really understood love. But if man ever really understood Jesus' meaning of love and *used* love what a different world we would have. What a revolution we would have if this were done! *This would be the ultimate revolution.* This would truly be the milennium - the true tapping in to the victorious Spirit which is in all men!

There is a great deal of difficulty experienced by most people who are attempting to practice the "loving of all creatures." Many times we meet people who are very difficult to like - then how do we mange to love them if it is difficult to even like them? "Loving" and "liking" are not necessarily the same thing. One must recognize that love (God) is in all, through all, with all. Love exists in all and one must view all with the certain knowledge that he is

74

The holy command to love.

(p man
reach
goal
of one
have
equated
him)

commanded to love others. In other words, we have "holy" orders to express love - this requires looking for the good; it requires no condemnation or if there has been condemnation, it requires forgiveness; it requires helping the individual to reach his goal; it requires that the individual be helped in reaching toward Spirit (which should be his and our goal!) In other words, it requires that one walk the second mile with that individual. These are the "holy" orders of love which we have received.

The "holy" order we have received in regard to "loving one another" is quite different from just "liking one another". We often like another because of mutual interests, sensory attachments, and because likes attract. This may have nothing to do with the "holy" orders to love one another. We may not feel a "liking" for someone *but* we must feel love for all - we must learn to do so. In loving we look for the good; we return good for evil; we set free the oppressed; we open the eyes of the spiritually blind; we do everything possible for the hungry, the sick, and the oppressed. Sometimes we don't always like them - we may not choose to be around them - but we love them because they, too, are of God.

Amazingly, though, if we really practice love - really manifest it - there will be very few we don't genuinely like. When we attempt to look for the good (the God perfection in others) - which means we are practicing the art of loving - we will very quickly discover that we end up liking the individual as well!

Doesn't loving make awfully good sense? If you make an attempt to love another he senses that and it will be very difficult for him to be negative toward you. When an individual feels understanding, acceptance, tolerance, brotherliness coming from another he is bolstered, strengthened and he then can express this feeling back. The more I give out this feeling the more I receive. *The only way to receive more love is to give more!*

I was given this little statement concerning the power of love to lead us to Spirit, and it is very meaningful to me:

The Spirit that was divided will be united. Love will stay united yet will be divided to be given to the still divided Spirit that all will be united.

This is a very beautiful statement and full of truth. Every being is a part of Spirit - man is searching for a meaning in life and that meaning is to advance, on the road back to pure Spirit. Love is the great unifying force in the universe - it can be divided again and again but by dividing it simply becomes more and more united (it multiplies by division.) When man was born he broke away from total Spirit - he became a separated part. Now his purpose in life must be to reunite with the total Spirit from which he was separated by birth. The only way man can be truly united - can truly regain the victorious Spirit - is through love! So as the little statement goes - the Spirit that was divided (man being separated at birth) will be united through the power of love (love was divided but is still united through the power of multiplication). Love will stay united yet will be divided to be given to the still divided Spirit (love because it cannot be diminished - only increased - by dividing becomes the unifying force for Spirit.) Then, *all* is united - the multiplying power of love to lead us to man's victorious Spirit!

In conclusion one might well consider a statement made by Teilard de Chardin:

"Someday, after mastering the winds, the waves,
the tides and gravity
We shall harness for God
the energies of love and then,
For a second time in the history of the world,
man will have discovered fire."

What a beautiful statement and what a true one! When mankind starts to seriously consider the multiplying power of love - the tremendous energy and power that lies latent - the great changes in the state of mankind will take place.

In a way it is so strange that love, the basic concept behind every great religion and especially our own, has been so little seriously studied by scholars other than those connected with philosophy or religion. Millions, even billions, have been spent on psychological research, on ships, airships, gravity, etc. - but practically nothing on love - the greatest power that has ever existed, or ever will exist.

When man finally realizes the multiplying power of

love - both from a physical and psychological standpoint - truly the world will be more revolutionized than it was with the discovery of fire, the combustible engine or atomic energy!

CHAPTER NINE

Freedom: The Gift

Nothing is more priceless than freedom. Freedom is an endowment of every soul. As Baltasar Gracian said, "Freedom is more precious than any gifts for which you may be tempted to give it up." Yet, of all things prized most by man few are more misunderstood than is the nature of freedom. So often man is concerned with "freedom to" do something usually of a materialistic nature. Man should be more concerned with "freedom of" or "freedom from" - "freedom of" or "from" the shackles he has placed on his own spirit, his own consciousness, his own free will. I believe one of the most important of all passages in the Bible is John 8:31-36: "Turning to the Jews who had believed Him, Jesus said, 'If you dwell within the revelation I have brought, you are indeed my disciples; you shall know the truth and the truth will set you free.' They replied, 'We are Abraham's descendants; we have never been in slavery to any man. What do you mean by saying, 'You will become free men?' 'In very truth I tell you', said Jesus, 'that everyone who commits sin is a slave. The slave has no permanent standing in the household, but the son belongs to it forever. If then the Son sets you free, you will indeed be free.'"

If, as Jesus said, he truly freed us, how do we lose our freedom? If freedom has been granted to us, why do so many of us feel "chained down" and feel that we are enslaved to our environment and forced by circumstances to a way of life which is anything but free?

Is it not true that of all tyrannies the greatest is the tyranny of the mind? What is meant by "tyranny of the

78

mind"? Is it not the loss of mental freedom? In fact, one should ask first what is meant by "freedom."

What I am really discussing - what Jesus really gave us - is freedom of the mind, *freedom to make a choice!*

The only real enslavement one can have is the enslavement of the mind. The enslavement of the mind one allows usually quite willingly. In fact, man normally does it to himself! The individual creates his own "tyranny of the mind."

Victor Frankl, the great existentalist psychologist, spent months in a Nazi death camp condemned to death; while there, he learned of the killing of many in his family. Yet, he states that for the first time in his life he found freedom, real freedom, while condemned in a death camp. This was possible for him, he tells us, because for the first time he became master of his own mind. He learned how to free himself! He learned of the victorious Spirit within every man! We should all read Victor Frankl's great story, *Man's Search for Meaning,* because it is a beautiful lesson in the ability of man to rise above his environment, circumstances, problems and imprisonment of the body and really become free!

In trying to understand the nature of true freedom one should attempt to determine how he becomes enslaved.

It is easy to understand how the body can become enslaved - there are such things as physical slavery, such things as enforced imprisonment, such things as political enslavement, etc. But how little most of us realize that there is mental enslavement because it is so much more common, so much more subtle and so much more effective! Yet, it is this mental enslavement from which Jesus clearly showed us the path to freedom!

For a fact most of the world lives in the most potent kind of enslavement even though all the great religions without exception, and I think especially Christianity, have taught us how to become truly free. We first become enslaved because we dwell only on the materialistic aspects of the world. We become hypnotized to "worldly" things. We become anesthetized by materialism. We see only the material and none of the great beauty that lies within ourselves and others. We forget that the "world was created out of things which do not appear."

Because we dwell on worldly things we develop a very

negative concept of life. We begin on our road to becoming enslaved by dwelling on the negatives of this world of which we are surrounded nearly all the time. In fact, one cannot listen to a news broadcast (which most of us do too many times a day), we cannot pick up a newspaper without becoming terribly negative in our outlook. However, I have often thought that we should look at our newspapers, our radio and television broadcasts a little differently than is our normal procedure. We should be happy - even joyous - that the newspapers and news broadcasts are so full of negatives. We should be joyful over the stories of riots, man's inhumanity to man, etc. because of the *nature* of news. (Of course, it would be wonderful if never in the world did any events of a negative nature occur.) For something to be really newsworthy (news) it must be unusual or unique. Therefore, when we think of the things that are in the news we should be thankful about the negatives found there because these negative events are still so unique or unusual as to be rated as newsworthy. It would be a rather horrible day if someday it became newsworthy whenever a kind deed was performed, whenever someone performed a kindly act or proposed an unselfish program, etc. It would mean that the kindly act or deed was so exceptional that it was newsworthy! However, we do not look at news media in this manner. We are consciously letting into our minds the negativity found in news and dwelling on all the unpleasant aspects never realizing what we are doing to our minds. By dwelling on the isolated event that is of a negative nature we are not being very practical, and certainly we are doing nothing of a constructive nature to our spirit - we are really destroying Spirit's freedom.

Through many avenues of our consciousness and even our unconscious we develop a habit of thinking of ourselves and of our world in the most materialistic and negative of ways. We hypnotize ourselves into believing the negatives about ourselves and our world and we create our reality from these negatives.

We accept as facts things that we have been exposed to - exposed to through our environment, through our education, through our experiences, through the news media, through authorities. How often this "exposure" has been incorrect! How often even authorities are quite wrong! Anyone who has been in a position where he is taken as an "authority" quickly develops a real feeling of humility - any professor can tell one very quickly that the more one learns about "facts" the more quickly he becomes aware of how much more there is to learn and how often previously accepted "facts" have proven incorrect! We often allow "authorities" in a certain subject area to become "jailers of our mind" in that area. One should look at the inventions and the breakthroughs in science and social science and see how many of these really important "breakthroughs" occurred because some individual did not lose his freedom to think or act creatively since he did not accept the statement from some "authority" that it was impossible! Would man have ever flown if some men had not had "free minds" in regard to flight - if authorities who gave very rational facts as to why flight was impossible had not been ignored? I certainly do not mean that in order to be free man must ignore all authorities in the various fields of endeavor. This would be the height of folly. What I am saying is that man must use his intuition, man must exercise his freedom of choice in selecting what he believes to be the truth.

If you believe anything enough it becomes a reality to you! If you accept anything that you hear then that is your reality. The only reality you hold or can hold is what you have allowed to be vividly imagined by yourself to be true. What you believe to be true *is* your reality. It has nothing to do with whether it is true or false, concrete or flimsy.

How often we misplace our belief! How often we have accepted something as a fact and later discovered, usually to our sorrow, that we did not have all the information, or we were looking at it from the wrong viewpoint, or we were even deliberately misled.

We are so easily hypnotized by the acceptance of "facts" that we have misperceived, misunderstood, or misinterpreted that it is no wonder we feel "hemmed in", "enslaved" or "imprisoned". *Especially,* if we have been dwelling only on the "facts" of a materialistic nature from this materialistic world. Materialistic "facts" are the very kind that we have been receiving from all media, from nearly all our education, and from our environment. I really have very little faith in the future of college education in America today. Practically the only thing that college education today is doing is activating certain sensory centers - it has nothing to do with developing man's Spirit. In fact, even the body is being pretty much ignored in college today. As long as the colleges dwell only on information and don't help man to develop an awareness of Spirit, we are in for trouble!

We must learn the importance of not allowing ourselves to become enslaved by worldly "facts", by materialistically conceived ideas about ourselves and our world. We must learn to allow the Spirit to free itself everyday! Every day we must free ourselves from the known.

Innocence should *not* be thought of as only innocence in the sexual sense - it is innocence of letting the world and its materialism (enslavement) become a major part of our "thinking". If we are to be free, *truly free,* we must harken to the words of Paul in II Corinthians 4:4, "Their unbelieving minds are so blinded by the gods of this passing age, that the gospel of the glory of Christ, who is the very image of God, cannot dawn upon them and bring them light."

To win freedom - real freedom - we must start being realistic about what really destroyed our "innocence", what really took away the freedom which God gave us. We will find the enslavement was the direct result of our allowing our images of the world and of ourselves to be formed through purely worldly (materialistic) things. *We enslaved and enslave ourselves!*

There is no basic argument with the "environmentalists" who tell us that our environment is the greatest determiner of what we become. They tell us that we are a product of our environment. This is true of most of us, *but it does not have to be true!*

One can find hundreds of examples of men from the same family, raised in exactly the same environment who are as different as night and day in terms of attitudes, accomplishments, morality, ability, etc. What has made the difference?

One has allowed the world (environment) to corrupt - to hypnotize him into feeling a certain way, to holding a certain image. The other has gone beyond his environment by allowing himself to be molded by higher thoughts - he has allowed the victorious Spirit to guide him. He has been "free from the known" which was his environment. The late, great Dr. Albert Schweitzer once said, "Man must cease attributing his problems to his environment, and learn again to exercise his will - his personal responsibility in the realm of faith and morals." Dr. Matthew N. Chappell, the well-known psychologist has said, "Happiness (a manifestation of freedom) is purely internal. It is produced not by objects, but by ideas, thoughts and attitudes which can be developed and constructed by the individual's own activities, irrespective of the environment."

Until man ceases to blame all his problems, all his enslavement, on his own environment and realizes that he has free will (that he is always free in his mind if he wishes) man will be enslaved - he will never be free.

Freudian psychologists hold the theory (a theory not shared by most Jungian psychologists and existentialists) that our basic drives - particularly our sexual drive - master us. They make us their slaves. In other words, some Freudians tell us that we are not "masters of our own fate" but are rather enslaved to the biological and psychological drives - that these drives destroy our freedom of action and thought. Again, there is no quarrel with the Freudians because as our society acts today (not just the Western world but the *whole* world) we have let our basic biological and psychological drives dominate us. We have allowed them dominion over us and we thereby become enslaved.

But this enslavement to biological and psychological drives is not necessary! It is in this area that we do have a quarrel with the Freudians. It has been determined in so many ways - with scientific proof - that the mind is much more powerful than the physical organs of the body. In other words, much more powerful than biological drives *if* we choose to exercise the power of the brain through controlling the thoughts we hold! However, as long as we dwell on worldly things - as long as we dwell on materialism - we will remain enslaved to our biological and psychological drives. Hence, since most of the world dwells on the material aspects of the world, the Freudians are correct. They are telling us the truth but only because we have *allowed* it to happen to us. But *fundamentally* they are wrong, they are not correct because man does have free will - he can control those other forces and so he can free himself if he chooses to do so. It is entirely up to him!

Such things as jealousy, envy, lying, greed, distrust, quarrelling, hating, complaining, etc. all serve to destroy freedom because all require that a negative attitude be adopted. When the mind starts moving "negatively" it starts seeing limitations for self and others with the result that one feels a loss of freedom. *One begins to challenge free will!*

We must begin to realize that under nearly all circumstances we can have dominion - complete dominion - over our mind. The only occasions when we cannot exercise complete dominion over the mind are when we are under the influence of alcohol, drugs or hypnosis. Under all other conditions *we have dominion over all aspects of ourselves - body, mind and spirit.* We can become completely free!! We must realize that the brain is a great storing apparatus - so great it is beyond human comprehension. Eminent scientists including neurophysisists have stated that billions of electronic cells would be needed to construct a facsimile of man's brain. Over a million cubic feet of space would be required for the cells and more millions of cubic feet would be needed for the wiring which would correspond to nerves! Power required to operate it would be beyond comprehension but would be in the hundreds of millions. Truly, beyond comprehension! *But we are programmers for that brain with its great potential! What we feed it makes it operate.* If we feed it on worldly things - which are mainly negative or of a selfish and egotistical nature - then it will program back to us (with great power) limitations, negativity, and, above all, the idea that we are not "masters" of our own fate. As we are told in Romans 12:2, "Adapt yourselves no longer to the pattern of this present world, but let your minds be remade and your whole nature thus transformed. Then you will be able to discern the will of God, and to know what is good, acceptable and perfect."

The analogy of programming the mind with the programming of the computer is an apt one. Computer programmers often use the expression, gigo. This expression is used to convey the idea that if the computer is programmed with poor, false or incorrect information, the computer will deliver back to the programmer poor, false or incorrect information - in other words, *garbage in, garbage out.* The computer can do nothing good with bad information or bad programming. In the case of mankind, if the mind is fed with the negatives of life and this world then as a result freedom is lost. If one puts limitations into consciousness one is going to limit his output. If one puts into his mind great spiritual truths he will get them back with more power and energy - with more certainty - than when he originally conceived them - the victorious Spirit that is within all human activates and increases the power of the spiritual truths that have been allowed to enter.

Many people believe in the law of "sowing and reaping" or the Law of Karma (both are very similar even though Karma implies reincarnation and "sowing and reaping" may not); and perhaps many will argue the question of "where is freedom when I must reap the whirlwind of what I did before?" Many believe in predestination and concepts similar to it. Here, too, it would be argued that there is no freedom when one is destined to meet a certain fate. Again, those who would argue along the line just indicated are dwelling on worldly things - dwelling on the materialistic level pure and simple. Man does have complete freedom in terms of how he accepts his karmic problems or "predestined hurdles." The attitude he adopts toward those problems, the love he expresses concerning the events and times in his life, is completely up to him. Of course, if he has let his environment, his biological and psychological drives and/or his worldly experiences dictate to him how problems shall be handled - if he dwells on the negative aspects of those problems - he is naturally *not* going to feel free.

If mankind wishes to recognize the fact that man creates his own personal environment and can drop the attitude of "worldliness" then man will be able to feel this marvelous ecstasy of freedom.

In I Peter 2:16 it is stated that if men wish to live as free men, they must live as servants of God. Man is being told that when he lives in Spirit (not in the materialistic world) he can truly live as a free man.

Free will in man is his right of choice. As applied to his relationship to God, it means that he has the privilege of choosing whether he will recognize and observe the Divine Law or try to live independently. The *only* real freedom in the world - for the emperor, the millionaire, the genius, the leader of many men, or the more ordinary mortal - rests in freedom of the Spirit. It rests in knowing the Truth - knowing the spiritual beauty, knowledge, and wealth that is within man; knowing that the material, worldly things all vanish; knowing that the only lasting values are concerned with spiritual and inter-personal and intra-personal relationships; knowing that love is the foundation of all lasting values. Truly, as Jesus told us, "You shall know the truth and the truth shall set you free."

The *real* freedom rests in acquiring the habit of realizing that it is looking through and to spiritual ideas - things of the Spirit - that true freedom can and will be found. True freedom will never be found in relying on worldly goods, worldly acts and worldly ideas. It is only through Spirit - going to our inner selves and inner concepts *un*influenced by materialism - that the real freedom is found. Man has been taught this idea from nearly the beginning of time; but he has rarely felt the ecstasy of freedom because he has been shackled by the materialism of the world, and he has been tyrannized by the mind that has been dwelling only on the so-called "facts" of the materialistic world in which he finds himself.

We are free when we know the Truth without any need for rationalization or justification - when we know that we know and no one can upset that knowledge. We must realize that in speaking of freedom we often confuse freedom "to" and freedom "of". *Man wants and must learn to be free "of" whatever he has created which keeps him from the greater force - Spirit.*

There is a price to pay to be completely free - it is the price of complete self-knowledge and growing to be what you want to be spiritually. One cannot have freedom without knowing self; one cannot know self until one knows what self is a part of; one cannot know what self is a part of until one knows from what self has been separated - and what one's self has been separated from is the all pervasive and victorious Spirit.

I choose to believe that the true lesson of Adam and Eve and the Garden of Eden, which in similar form appears in so many religions, is that man lost his "innocence" when he chose to live by worldly laws rather than by spiritual law. I believe that when man placed his sensory desires above his spiritual knowledge he lost his innocence and fell from grace. It is in the giving up of the desires of a worldly nature and going back to the spiritual law that man regains his innocence and his freedom.

To be free of the bondage of self we must learn to drop the personality (something which is purely of this world.) The giving up of the personality is the price that must be paid. The personality is a product of environment, the sensory system, worldly drives and ambitions, psychological desires, etc. When we chose to be born we chose to be bound. As we grow in understanding we can grow toward being free - we learn to break the bonds of limitation. This *is* the lesson of the earth incarnation - to become free by reuniting with pure Spirit. Then the victory is won!

However, breaking the bonds of limitation is not easy because as we begin to realize the importance of attempting to reunite with pure Spirit everything that has happened to us, everything that we have relied upon suddenly loses much of its significance. Suddenly we feel not freedom but rather we feel as though everything is crushing in on us and that our world is collapsing. We feel as though what we are doing is impractical. But the lesson of this incarnation is to become free by reuniting with pure Spirit which means the dropping of all products of environment, the sensory system, worldly drives, psychological drives, etc. This requires making a very great break - making a very great change in our mode of living and thinking. Change - or even a transition period - is always difficult for man because he feels a loss of security due to knowledge of the "old" or past and lack of knowledge of the "new" or future. But when man starts "feeding his mind" with things of the Spirit (love, high ideals, patience, understanding) he suddenly emerges from his days of darkness during the change and becomes aware of the great light which is found in understanding and reuniting with the great, victorious Spirit.

Paul stated in Romans 8:2, "In Christ Jesus the life-giving law of the Spirit has set you free from the law of sin and death." In Galatians 5:1 Paul said, "Christ set us free, to be free men." Only man, through the misuse of his mind, can make himself lose the freedom that has been given to him. Man has the free will to either accept his freedom or choose the enslavement.

By exercising free will through "going within", through holding non-worldly ideas concerning our condition and the condition of others, and through our attempting to reunite with Spirit we find the *real freedom!*

CHAPTER TEN

Creativity and Constructive Thought:
The Manifestations

Two very challenging and important passages in the Bible are Proverbs 23:7 - "For as he thinketh in his heart, so *is* he" and Romans 12:2 - "Adapt yourselves no longer to the pattern of this present world, but let your minds be remade and your whole nature thus transformed."

Current psychological understanding, clinical work and other scientific research reveals the great wisdom of both these passages. More and more we can prove that the attitudes (thoughts) we hold concerning things, ideas, concepts, etc. *determine what we are!* Our attitudes determine the good and the bad that come to us. Our attitudes determine the material, the physical, the spiritual and the mental condition in which we find ourselves. As Einstein so aptly put it: "The most beautiful and most profound emotion we can experience is the sensation of the mystical. It is the sower of all true science. He to whom this emotion is a stranger, who can no longer wonder and stand rapt in awe, is as good as dead. To know that what is impenetrable to us really exists, manifesting itself as the highest wisdom and the most radiant beauty which our dull faculties can comprehend only in their most primitive forms - this knowledge, this feeling is at the center of true religiousness."* It is becoming more and more apparent that man must spend more time in the "playhouse of his mind" to use the expression of Dr. Maxwell Maltz in

The Universe and Dr. Einstein, by Lincoln Barnett,
William Morrow Company, 1948

89

*Psycho-Cybernetics*** in alluding to the importance of vividly imagining the good - of vividly imagining the accomplishment of our goals.

We are abundantly aware, again through scientific studies, that the brain and nervous system do not know the difference between what is vividly imagined and reality. If we hold the attitude of expected failure, or the attitude that we probably cannot succeed because we have failed before or don't have the attributes of someone else who has succeeded then we shall have failure, we shall have depression, we will allow the creative mechanism to wither and die.

Who does not believe that his body responds to the type of nourishment - food, drink and shelter - he provides? Who does not recognize the importance of proper nourishment for plant and animal life? Surely all are in agreement that proper nourishment is essential to healthy life. There are various schools of thought as to just what is the proper "diet" for each type of life; but essentially all agree that diet, protection from certain elements, and reasonable liquid intake are necessary for biological development. But how few of us recognize that just as vital to healthy and abundant life are uplifting, positive thoughts! The world of science has recorded innumerable experiments which prove beyond any doubt that thought has a definite bearing on our physical well-being. Some experiments indicate that certain types of vibrations (and thoughts) have a relationship to the health of other forms of animal and plant life as well.

None of the scientific experiments concerning the importance of thought should surprise a student of Biblical works, or of the works of Buddha, Krishna, and others. In Proverbs 3 we read:

"All the ways of a man are pure in his own eyes;
but the Lord weighs the spirit.
Commit your work to the Lord,
and your plans will be established."

Jesus said: "Do you not see that whatever goes into the mouth passes into the stomach, and so passes on? But what comes out of the mouth proceeds from the heart, and

***Psycho-Cybernetics,* Maxwell Maltz, Prentice-Hall Co., 1960

this defiles a man. For out of the beast come bad thoughts, murder, adultery, fornication, theft, false witness, slander. These are what defile a man; but to eat with unwashed hands does not defile a man." Our great religious teachers of the past and the present have been telling us that our thoughts have a direct bearing on both our physical and mental well-being. Now science is emphasizing this fact in many ways.

It is a fact that the nervous system reacts through "imaginings" just as it reacts during the actual happening. How are we nourishing our body when we think in terms of doing harm to others - failure, revenge, and the like? It is rather frightening to realize that when we watch television and "live" through the violence, hatred, revenge, and greed depicted so often on the screen, our nervous system responds to a great degree just as though we ourself were living these experiences!

The more we vividly imagine negatively (as we usually do in regard to envy, hate, and jealousy), the more likely we are to be mal-nourishing ourself. To gain nourishment we must make those "vivid images" into loving, beautiful ones. When we belittle ourselves, when we dwell on past failures and mistakes, we are setting up a pattern that will assure us of failures and mistakes in the future. We are "imagining" ahead in the most negative of ways. By belitting ourself and our ability, we are in a very real sense belittling God's goals and God's gift to each man of special, individual talents and abilities. Paul wrote: "For if any one thinks he is something, when he is nothing, he deceives himself. But let each one test his own work, and then his reason to boast will be in himself alone and not in his neighbor. For each man will have to bear his own load."

We usually dwell on failure in terms of some "image" we hold of some specific person and we feel we do not measure up to that individual. It is fine to have people we admire and appreciate, but we should recognize that admiring another is not the same thing as trying to *be* that other person. Each of us has his own capabilities, his own pathway, his own talents, burdens, and problems; as Jesus said so many times and in so many ways, each of us is unique. However, the true uniqueness comes in the thought process (all of us are "atomically" the same), and no man can live another man's thoughts. If he tries, he is doomed to failure with consequent unfortunate reactions in mind and body. It reminds me of the story of the six-year-old who was asked by a relative what he wanted to be; the child replied; "I would like to be myself. I tried to be other things, but I always failed." What a wise child!

Planting the seed of failure in our own thoughts (or even worse, in someone else's mind) is truly taking nourishment from the body. Experiment after experiment conducted under scientific circumstances has demonstrated that when a person is repeatedly told he is a failure, or thinks of himself as a failure, the mechanism for failure is established. In one of his syndicated columns in September, 1968, Dr. Alfred A. Messer reported on a fascinating study performed with children:

"at the beginning of a school year, teachers were told that they could expect a spurt in IQ from certain of the youngsters. (The teachers were given fictitious test scores for these youngsters.) When tested at the end of the school year, the children who had been selected at random as 'intellectual bloomers' actually did show a spurt in IQ....Not only can the teacher's attitude influence his response to the child, but he unwittingly can convey the same set of expectancies to the youngster. Soon enough the...child may begin to think of himself as someone who can't keep up, or someone who is destined to 'flunk.' This kind of expectancy can pertain to any school child. The child who has had psychiatric treatment for emotional problems is often 'expected' to cause trouble. Whenever a disturbance occurs in the classroom, the teacher may automatically look in his direction. The child, sensing that he is expected to make trouble, can learn to oblige his teacher."

Dr. William Parker, who wrote "Prayer Can Change Your Life," and other outstanding authorities tell us that the problem of the stutterer is usually a problem of parental "thought" injection to the child (except in those cases of definite physiological disorders.) The average parent, if he sees he child stumble when learning to crawl or walk, does not tell the child he is a stumbler, nor does he tell a child he is unable to eat right if he has trouble learning to use his eating utensils. But the same parent may become horrified when a child is unable to pick the proper word to express a thought - and the parent may say, "You are stuttering!" Frequently, if a child repeats the attempt to find the right word, the parent will identify him as a stutterer. The seed is sown, and the child in his thinking identifies *himself* as a stutterer; after all, he believes what his parent says and wants to please him. The "thought" of the parent, transferred to the child, has created a most unpleasant situation.

In order to solve the problem it is necessary to have the child *think* of himself differently - to stop thinking of himself as a stutterer. He has to eradicate an "image" of himself that has been given to him through the thought process of his parent. Perhaps it is not strange to find that the average stutterer is likely to be above average IQ: he has a larger vocabulary from which to select words, and this makes it more difficult to select immediately the right words for what he wants to express.

Dr. Joshua Lederberg, in his column in the San Francisco Chronicle in December, 1968, reported an experiment conducted at Rockefeller University by Doctors Leo DiCara and Neal Miller. To quote in part: "Their earlier work had established that rats could be trained, with reinforcement by electric stimulation to change their heart rate either up or down in response to a tone signal. In one of their most spectacular experiments, they showed that the rats could regulate a difference in blood flow to the right ear vs. the left ear, and without changing blood flow in other parts of the body. Dr. Miller and his colleagues have also shown 'learned' responses in kidney function and in contractions of the intestine. These experiments show beyond doubt that neutral circuits exist by which the brain can influence body functions long held to be autonomous."

In another column, Lederberg makes these statements: "Recent work on the experimental psychology of laboratory animals has focused renewed attention on the mutual relationship of bodily states and emotional disturbances as a central factor in mental health. The medical profession and the interested public has, by now, become reasonably perceptive about psychosomatic disease: the extent to which emotional unbalance can distort bodily functions and eventually produce such gross pathology as a bleeding ulcer."

After all, emotional disturbances are thought disturbances. We should examine a little more closely the word *disease*. If we take it apart, we find "dis" and "ease" - the lack of being at ease. With what are we not at ease? Probably something in our environment, our body, or (and most likely) our thoughts. In many cases our lack of positiveness and love in our thoughts has prevented us from being "at ease," and we have developed an unhealthy mind or body, or mind *and* body. We have not given our body the proper thought nourishment.

When we think of nourishing our victorious Spirit as well as our body, we should keep in mind what Paul meant when he said God is all over, through all, in all. Surely he did not mean just in the atoms of matter, but in the energy of thought as well. Science today makes it easy for us to see the tremendous power of energy (the laser beam is one example); and when one realizes that thought is a form of energy, it becomes obvious that our thoughts are a major factor in our total nourishment. Negative thoughts create negative conditions, and thoughts of love and truth and understanding create healthy conditions, in mind and body.

We must learn to recognize that each of us was created with special aptitudes, abilities, limitations; but all of us are given the ability to perform well. As we read in I Corinthians 12:5,6,7: "There are varieties of service, but the same Lord; and there are varieties of working, but it is the same God who inspires them all in every one. To each is given the manifestation of the Spirit for the common good." The teachings of Jesus make it abundantly clear that if we are to have an abundant, healthy physical life we must feed ourself with abundant, loving, healthful thoughts. Science is confirming what the scriptures of all the basic religions have told us.

Most of us spend our time in a vain struggle to cope with the problems of the world - quite often problems over which we could never have any control or even personal involvement. We pick up the newspaper or watch the news broadcast and our nervous system gets "up tight" because we are being exposed to the chaos and misery of the world. We are not told of the many wonderful things that are going on - for every riot, for every murder, for every antagonistic act we see or read about we are not told that there are probably millions of kindnesses being shown by people, millions of acts of unselfishness being performed, millions of honest, dedicated, sincere people working to bring about good in their and our world. But the press is geared to the sensational, to the negative - to news. We should realize that *it is news* when major chaos, major calamities occur. However, when we dwell on the negative news, which most of it is, we are forming attitudes that cause us to be depressed, to be negative toward life and people. We are affecting our body, our mind and our spirit in a very unhealthy way. Again, our nervous system does not know the difference between what we vividly imagine is happening and what is actually happening.

When we dwell on worldly things we are ignoring the spirit side of life and the great spiritual uplift that is possible for us at all times. As is stated in Romans 12:2 - "Adapt yourselves no longer to the pattern of the present world, but let your minds be remade and your nature thus transformed." How clearly Paul is telling us that we must not let our minds dwell on the negatives of this world. We must not form our attitudes toward life and spirit from the worldly side. If we form our attitudes toward life from purely worldly things, we are naturally going to have a negative, pessimistic, depressing spirit consciousness. If we want to be happy, to be loving, to have a spiritual awakening, then we must remake our minds along spiritual lines and thereby our whole nature will be transformed. This suggestion is a good scientific principle because the only meaning anything has is the meaning you give it! Nothing has meaning until you have an attitude toward it. This can be demonstrated in so many ways - for example, to a Frenchman snails are one of the world's real delicacies, to the average Anglo-Saxon the idea of a snail as food is really most revolting (attitude!); to a native Chinese certain types of birds' nests are a delicacy, to most of us birds' nests would be most un-appetizing; to most of us catsup is a very fine addition to many foods, yet to many races it is most unpleasant. Why the difference when the "reality" of the food is the same? The difference is due to differing attitudes - attitudes that have been formed at some time in life toward specific food items. We could find the same differences among various cultures in regard to such things as marriages, homes, streets, animals, etc. etc. In all cases, the food, the marriage, the home, the street, the animal, etc. has the same outer appearance but our attitude tells us whether it is beautiful, ugly, disagreeable, pleasant, etc.

If we look within we quickly discover that the attitudes we have of a negative nature were formed by the "pattern of this present world" - by paying attention to "worldly" things and ignoring our spiritual side. We have dwelt too long over news reports, illness, financial problems, job experiences, etc. We have not taken the time to discover the wonderful inner and hidden beauty of much of the world and of the people we know. As Rachel Carson so beautifully put it in *The Sense of Wonder:** "For most of us, knowledge of our world comes largely through sight, yet we look about with such unseeing eyes that we are partially blind! We look too hastily, seeing the whole and not its parts. Children, perhaps because they themselves are small and closer to the ground, notice and delight in the small and inconspicuous. A child's world is fresh and new, full of wonder and excitement. If I had influence with the good fairy who is supposed to preside over the christening of all children I should ask her gift to each child in the world be a sense of wonder so indestructible that it would last throughout life, as an unfailing antidote against the boredom and disenchantment of later years - the sterile preoccupation with things that are artificial - the alienation from the sources of our strength."

In following the admonition of Paul in Romans 12:2 that we adapt ourselves to the pattern of this present world, we don't ignore the world - we just need to see the beauty in the world, its people and within ourselves. Certainly looking for beauty and dwelling on the inner peace is *not* following the pattern of the present world. Charles Lindbergh in a beautiful article, "A Letter from Lindbergh",** in *Life* magazine in July, 1969, very wonderfully put forth this same thesis. In part he said: "I believe early entrance to this era (space age) can be attained by the application of our scientific knowledge not to life's mechanical vehicles but to the essence of life itself:

**The Sense of Wonder,* Rachel Carson, Harper-Row, 1965

**From "A Letter From Lindbergh", by Charles A. Lindbergh, *Life* Magazine, July 7, 1969   c   1969 Time Inc.

to the infinite and infinitely evolving qualities that have resulted in awareness, shape and character of man. I believe this application is necessary to the very survival of mankind." He went on to say, "...Through his (man's) evolving awareness, and his awareness of that awareness, he can merge with the miraculous - to which we can attach what better name than 'God'? And in this merging, as long sensed by intuition but still only vaguely perceived by rationality, experience may travel without need for accompanying life.

"Will we then find life to be only a stage, though an essential one, in a cosmic evolution of which our evolving awareness is beginning to become aware? Will we discover that only *without* spaceships can we reach galaxies; that only *without* cyclotrons can we know the interior of atoms? To venture beyond the fantastic accomplishments of this physically fantastic age, sensory perception must combine with the extrasensory, and I suspect that the two will prove to be different faces of each other. I believe it is through sensing and thinking about such concepts that great adventures of the future will be found."

Certainly, Lindbergh, one of our truly great explorers and scientists, is telling us that the world within may be far more interesting, far more challenging, far more revealing than the world without. In a way Lindbergh seems to me to be saying almost what Paul said in 2 Corinthians 4:4, "Their unbelieving minds are so blinded by the god of this passing age, that the gospel of the glory of Christ, who is the very image of God, cannot dawn upon them and bring them light." We must take the time to look other than at the "pattern of this present world" and form an attitude of acceptance for the beauty that is within both ourselves and nature.

We have to realize that nothing has meaning until we form an attitude toward it. Nothing can bother us until we have formed a negative attitude toward it. If our attitudes toward life and spirit are formed solely through worldly knowledge, then most of our attitudes will be very unhealthy. Most of our education, most of our communication media, most of our exposure is to the negatives of life and so negative attitudes toward all things become predominant with us. This is why Paul asked us so strongly to adapt ourselves from within and truly our natures will be transformed. Let us look at some attitudes all of us could work with - or at least some things we could avoid in order to form a better attitude toward life and Spirit - so we could remake our minds and let our natures be transformed.

a. We must realize that it is our attitude toward a job or project at the *beginning* which will determine its ultimate outcome. The mind is a goal striving mechanism and it does not know the difference between imagined and actual failure. So if we start a task with a feeling of fear or negativity of any kind the job will be difficult, if not impossible, to complete. Remember, it is your attitude toward the job that makes it difficult or relatively easy - it is not the job that creates the problem or provides the answer!

b. We must remember that our attitude toward life will create for us what life is! Life, as such, has no meaning except as we give it meaning. If we give it a negative meaning, we get that reflected back. If we approach life full of Spirit and love and understanding, we will have that reflected back. We should remember the Golden Rule in forming our attitude - Do unto others as you would have them do unto you. It is a basic law in forming our attitudes.

c. We should attempt to radiate a feeling of well being, of confidence, of sincerity. If we radiate such a feeling, people will form an attitude toward us of a person to whom trust can be given and to whom love can be freely expressed. This in turn will make our task easier and will bring love and understanding to us. Everyone becomes impatient with the constantly complaining, constantly depressed, constantly sorrowful person. Instead of understanding, that person often receives pity which is the very opposite of what is needed to build a spiritually healthy nature.

d. We must form the attitude of thinking of ourselves as uniquely created by God and realize that each of us has certain attributes and certain limitations - everyone is unique. We must walk, talk, act and conduct ourselves with confidence - not arrogance - but confidence in the fact that each is one of God's creations and unique. It is all right for us to have heroes and people we greatly admire. *But* we must realize that they, too, are unique and they are not we and we are not they. Too often we place someone we admire on a pedestal and we observe all his accomplishments and we see all his successful attributes, but we fail to see the problems that person has and the obstacles he has had to overcome to be where he is. We then look at ourselves from the standpoint of what we don't have that he has. As a result we are apt to think of ourselves in terms of limitations, in terms of attributes we don't possess, of failures that we have had. We always come out second best and we get into the habit of thinking of ourselves as failures, or as not having much potential for the future. We form a negative attitude about ourselves. Let us walk, talk and act with confidence no matter what position we hold in life knowing that each is unique and each has his mark to make in the spiritual realm! God did not make failures, nor did he create inferior persons or jobs or positions - only our attitude toward ourselves and toward our work can make us failures or inferiors because each individual and each job is unique.

e. People form an attitude toward us by reflecting the attitude we have toward them. If we are arrogant, if we hold an attitude of inferiority, superiority or dislike, we will have this reflected right back at us. The lesson here is the Golden Rule perhaps expressed in the following manner: "Have the attitude toward others that you would have them have toward you." We must remember that all people are inter-dependent and we have to make them feel at ease before we can feel at ease.

f. We must recognize that the mind entertains - and can entertain - only one thought at a time. If our attitude is one of reluctance, one of fear, one of dislike, one of doubt then this negative attitude becomes the prevailing thought. How can we become successful if we are full of doubt or fear? We must vividly imagine our goal, do the very best we can and not entertain the seed of failure which is lack of confidence in our own unique ability. We should often repeat and believe the following statement: "Divine order is established in my mind, body and affairs." This is the attitude we must adopt completely whenever we enter into a new task or when we are thinking about ourselves and our own self-image.

g. We must learn not to use gossip in a negative way and most gossip is negative. When one really thinks about it, gossip is usually a malicious thing and results from self-doubt. If we had a good image of ourselves, felt confident in our work and actions, had no fear or worry concerning what others thought of us, there would be no need for the negative type of gossip. Jungian psychologists tell us that most people who become gossips do so because of inadequacies they feel in themselves; and therefore, they take solace in the misfortune and peccadillos of others. If we would form the attitude toward ourselves that God created each of us uniquely there would be no psychological need to tear down either ourselves or others. We should not bother to waste our time telling others our personal problems and being relayers of bad news. Certainly giving voice to problems only intensifies those problems - it further ingrains on the consciousness the problem (it is a form of vividly imagining negatively which only creates an even greater problem.) Most of us are very much aware of the psychological evidence of the damage done by constantly dwelling on problems. Instead of broadcasting our problems we should see and vividly imagine the perfect solution and then "let go and let God" - turn it over to our victorious Spirit.

h. There is probably no area in life where people more abuse positive thought and affirmation than in the field of health. One should not talk about his health unless it is abundantly good - and then only in moderation. The teachings of many both in theology and medicine

100

are full of evidence of the problems created by dwelling on health problems. The medical profession estimates that fully sixty per cent of all illness is psychosomatic - induced by emotional disturbances. Psychosomatic illness results from mental imagining of a negative nature! If you have a slight headache or some other minor problem, see how much greater you can make the pain and misery by complaining about this to your friends and relatives! You can see the Law at work very quickly! If you feel the need of medical help, seek it out but don't broadcast the condition of your health to others - you will pay a great penalty if you broadcast your unhappy condition. Again, by being negative about it you are fixing an attitude toward your health which your nervous system does not know is not the "real thing". Likewise, when you see another person who may have been sick or looks "sickly" don't tell him how he has failed or how poorly he appears. This may be one time in life when a "white lie" will be valuable. If you must make some remark about his health say how happy you are to see him looking this well or that he is certainly improved from the last time you saw him. Don't make the man who may have suffered a great deal have the added burden of overcoming an "attitude" of sickliness which you may have given him. How much better if you said nothing about his physical condition! It is probably true that some people "enjoy poor health" but let us not encourage these people - they are seeking attention because of the poor attitude they have concerning their ability to communicate with others except through pity.

i. Let us start looking for the root causes of our negative attitudes and rid ourselves of them. Whenever we come upon a situation, a problem, a person, or something about ourselves we don't like or which we fear, let us see if we can find a way of looking at it differently. Let us see if we can change our attitude toward it. Will Rogers once said he never met a man he didn't like. This doesn't tell us much about the people he met but it tells us a great deal about Will Rogers.

He made it a point to look for something good in everyone he met - even if it meant focusing on some small physical feature of the person. Will Rogers approached a person with the attitude that there was something to like about everyone. How much more appropriate to use Will Rogers' approach than the approach so many of us use - we will find some feature or mannerism or even clothing someone is wearing that we don't like and then we dislike the individual because of that! Let us turn it around and see if we cannot form the habit of looking for something good in or about everyone we meet - this merely requires a change of attitude.

including ourselves

Through this discussion of attitude I have been trying to convey the idea that we create the image that we hold toward our world, toward people *and* toward ourselves by virtue of the attitudes we hold. We literally create us! Nothing has meaning except as our attitude gives it meaning. Any object, any thing, any being, any idea has no meaning - no existence - until we create it by giving it a meaning for ourselves! Hence, if we hold negative attitudes toward our ability, toward our physical attributes, toward our spiritual potential we will have created a very limited being. If we hold to positive affirmations concerning our uniqueness, our ability to progress spiritually, our ability to complete whatever tasks God has given us, our value as a person, then we create an individual who is truly able to fulfill his spiritual role in this world and one who can rise to Christ consciousness. *Literally, through out attitudes we create us;* or as it is so beautifully put in Proverbs 23:7, "For as he thinketh in his heart, so *is* he." Our creativity and our power of constructive thinking are only limited by our attitude - especially our attitude in regard to the divine nature of Spirit.

CHAPTER ELEVEN

Happiness: The Product

Abraham Lincoln once said that people are just about as happy as they make up their minds to be.

Lincoln, I believe, was telling us that happiness is a state of mind - it comes from a feeling of freedom, a feeling of love for those around us, a love of our environment, from a propensity to see good in all. Happiness is purely an internal (inside) matter - it comes to us from realizing the good in all - in other people, in all of God's creation, in ourselves. It is a state of mind! It has nothing to do with the acquisition of things whether they be worldly objects or objects of worldly admiration.

I believe that one of the greatest passages of scripture concerning happiness - or joy - is to be found in Isaiah 55:6-12:

"Inquire of the Lord while he is present,
call upon him when he is close at hand.
Let the wicked abandon their ways
and evil men their thoughts:
let them return to the Lord, who will
have pity on them,
return to our God, for he will freely
forgive.
For my thoughts are not your thoughts,
and your ways are not my ways.
This is the very word of the Lord.
For as the heavens are higher than the
earth,
so are my ways higher than your ways

and my thoughts than your thoughts;
and as the rain and the snow came down
from heaven
and do not return until they have
watered the earth,
making it blossom and bear fruit,
and give seed for sowing and bread
to eat,
so shall the word which comes from my
mouth prevail;
it shall not return to me fruitless
without accomplishing my purpose
or succeeding in the task I gave it.
*You shall indeed go out with joy
and be led forth in peace."*

We are most assuredly being told that joy, happiness, can be secured by dwelling on Truth, by expecting the best from the unknown, by realizing that God's good is always ready and waiting for us.

In studying world religions one is inevitably struck by the great similarity among the roots of all great beliefs - the necessity for love, the necessity for self-realization and self-respect, the necessity to realize the basic truth and justice of the law of sowing and reaping, etc. But one is also struck by one very fundamental difference between Christianity and most of the Eastern religions - in Christianity there is a great emphasis on joy and enthusiasm and on how suffering (unhappiness) can be avoided by following Truth. In some Eastern religions there is an emphasis on the necessity of suffering (unhappiness) in order to come into divine wisdom or Truth.

I believe it is in the teaching - the word - of Jesus wherein he gave the manner in which one can achieve spiritual understanding with joy and happiness that Christianity is superior to most other faiths. I certainly mean nothing disparaging about other religions - all have great basic truths. But Jesus taught man how to deliver himself from his suffering - told us why suffering is not necessary - whereas some of the other faiths emphasize suffering as *the* way to spiritual understanding, happiness and man's victorious Spirit.

Yet, strange as it may seem, Christianity, as a formal

religion, at times in the history of its churches has made "happiness" somehow seem to be evil. Often those expressing joy were somehow seen as immoral. How often in churches do we see people smile or laugh? How many laws still exist on the books in many states making it a crime to laugh or to enjoy oneself on Sundays - even thought these laws are fortunately no longer enforced? These laws were passed at the instigation of puritanical church groups! We have much in the literature of nearly all Christian sects which seems to indicate that somehow man must realize that being happy is not a very moral thing to be! What utter nonsense! Happiness is not a moral issue - it is not moral or immoral - it is amoral. Happiness is strictly a state of mind, and I believe it can best be achieved through understanding and living in spiritual truth - through attempting to reunite with the great purifying God force that is within us all - man's victorious Spirit. Happiness is a God-given right *but* we must activate this God-given right ourselves. As with any gift, or any right, *without the acceptance or the use*, it is as though the gift or the right never existed! In Nehemiah 8:10 it is written, "The joy of the Lord is your strength." If we claim the joy of the Lord as our strength aren't we also claiming joy for ourselves? Weariness, despair, loneliness, depression can be vanished from our lives *if* we are willing to recognize that the Lord's joy is our joy just as it is our strength. Of course to make this "recognition" come about requires that we really affirm and reaffirm our belief in the power, the strength, and the energy in the all-creative force of Spirit. It requires that we truly become practicing, believing disciples of the Christ Consciousness.

Ralph Waldo Emerson said that a man cannot be happy and strong until he too lives with nature in the present, above time. Emerson is telling us that we must live in the "now" and not keep postponing our happiness. We must learn to recognize the beauty and the joy in nature - in all nature (remember, you are very much a part of nature!) We must learn to look upon the world around us with positive attitudes and not look for the bad or the negatives. Happiness is strictly an "inside" job - it comes from a propensity to look for the good and to see the good in all situations and things. Paul told us in Romans 14:14, "I am absolutely convinced, as a Christian, that nothing is impure in itself; only, if a man considers a particular thing impure, then to him it is impure." When we dwell on all the evils we can find in our world, all the injustices done to us, all the slights in our lives, all the material things we do not have, we naturally feel no happiness - we are looking for the impurities and we are creating the impurities by our looking, our attitude. This causes us to lose our zest for life, causes us to feel oppressed and "put upon". If we took the time to look about us at the beauty of others, the beauty to be found in all things, for the good in all thoughts - and especially for the good in ourselves - we would have great joy, we would have great happiness. We have to quit thinking and saying, "oh, if only I had that I would be happy", or "if only he would do that, it would bring me such joy" or "next month I will be happy because I have a vacation", or I am so happy today is almost over, what a mess."

Whenever we look for happiness in the future we are apt to be greatly disappointed in that future and we are not going to have happiness *now!* We must start looking for the joy in the things, the situation, the people, in ourselves, *NOW!* When we keep expecting happiness in the future we are failing to look for the great beauty and purity in what is there right now - we have a tendency to look (focus) on the obstacles to that happiness *of* the future. We start dwelling on the obstacles to our future happiness and we are apt to become quite miserable now. We must start looking for something good - joyous in the situation that is currently with us. We must begin to recognize, as we are told, that the joy of the Lord is our strength - the Lord created all things and we must seek the joy in all things ourselves and we must do it currently. If the Lord found joy in all things who are we to find less than that in those things? When we start looking for the "non-joyous" aren't we trying to refute the Lord? After all he found joy in all creation. We must start living in the joyous and happy present and stop postponing our happiness to the future.

It is time man recognized that "waiting for" it to happen is not realistic in regard to happiness. Happiness does not occur "because of" anything! Happiness manifests itself when we are willing to open our minds to the present and to the good that is around us *Now.* Most of us get into the position of looking for happiness to come to us "because" something is going to happen, "because" some problem will be resolved, "because" we are to meet someone, etc. Actually when we are waiting for happiness "because of something" we are really destroying our chances for happiness - we are always in a "waiting process" for our happiness because there will always be problems, there will always be unpleasant situations, etc. Hence, we never become truly "happy". We may find a modicum of joy and happiness in a certain upcoming event, or in owning a certain thing, or meeting a certain person but that is a temporary process and so we enjoy happiness only for a very limited period of time; but we don't live in a state of happiness. We live waiting from one special event after another; and if they don't occur with great frequency we are apt to live a life full of suspended happiness and very little real happiness.

Again, we must start looking for the happiness *Now* in all the things, ideas and people around us. We must recognize that they are all God's creations so there must be purity and joy in all of them - sometimes it takes some "looking" but it is there!

How very often we think that if we are successful *then* we will be happy! Actually, success follows happiness and not vice versa. We become successful when we are happy - success *never* was a cause, per se, of happiness. No one who has been successful in any endeavor was completely unhappy while involved in that endeavor. In fact, nearly all the great artists, writers, inventors, "idealists" were extremely happy in their endeavor long before they achieved success. While involved in their "projects" they had a goal, they were looking for the good in what they were doing - they were observing what was right in their world. They were dwelling on the good - the purity - in what they were doing. All of us have read biographies and autobiographies of the great creative men and most of them suffered greatly from worldly problems while working on their projects (think of the starving artist!) *But* all of them seemed to be almost sublimely happy while working because they were working at what they enjoyed doing - they were full of enthusiasm for their work, they were *seeing the beauty and the good in the Now!*

Happiness is something you can create in your life *and* only you can do it for you! It comes through living in the present (looking for the good Now) and it comes through having a meaningful goal - a very real, very basic objective for your life. I truly believe the very best formula for happiness is to establish as your goal the raising of your spiritual awareness to where you become enlightened with Christ Consciousness - the return to your victorious Spirit. In having such a goal one quickly realizes that there is much in the present he must learn to appreciate, to understand, and to love before he can attain real growth on his ladder to Christ Consciousness - the return to his victorious Spirit. In having such a goal one quickly realizes that there is much in the present he must learn to appreciate, to understand, and to love before he can attain real growth on his ladder to Christ Consciousness. He becomes acutely aware of the present and he has established a goal that will always be meaningful to him.

The great creators in our society always have meaningful goals whatever their work, and they always have great faith in themselves to achieve in their field. They are living in the Now, and they are bound to find happiness because they are looking for the good in the present. I don't think it is unrealistic to say that nearly all great creative people have been very happy before they succeeded in the world's eyes. But it is astounding how many successful people, from the world's viewpoint, have been very unhappy *after* they succeeded. One reads so much of the unhappiness of the famed movie "stars", famed writers, famed artists, even of the suicides of very famous ones. Could their worldly success have brought them happiness? Obviously it did not. Happiness consists in finding beauty here and now - it is a mental state, as Emerson said, where there is a propensity to find good in all.

Success is not going to bring any happiness, per se. Success is much more apt to occur if one is happy, but success is not going to bring happiness unless the individual has established meaningful life goals and unless the individual has been able to live in the Now with joy and enthusiasm. Of course, "success" is normally judged from a "worldly viewpoint" and has little, if anything, to do with inner understanding where real success lies. We must stop feeling "I will be happy when I have finished this project", or "when I have succeeded." This is unrealistic. The successful conclusion of the project will not bring happiness - in fact, unless another goal is established almost immediately it may well do just the opposite. Happiness requires that we be enthusiastic over whatever we are doing; and we can be enthusiastic if we look for the good in what exists around us now.

All of us have seen the joy and happiness that a child can find in the little things around him - have you ever watched a small child with a rock or a stick or even a dead flower and seen the joy, enthusiasm, happiness he finds in that object? He is seeing the beauty in what to our more sophisticated eyes does not exist. We must learn to go back to the source of our real strength - which is the source of our happiness - and that strength is in realizing the great beauty in what the Lord has created. We must cease our constant postponement of happiness until some worldly event occurs in our lives. We must rejoice and be happy in the fact that we have been given the faculty to choose happiness or unhappiness - it is our choice because we do have free will.   We have the free will to select and concentrate on the negatives in our present life and in the things around us, and we will be unhappy. Or we have the free will to select and concentrate on the positives in our present life and in the things around us, and we will be happy. It is entirely up to us - it is purely "an inside job."

I know it is easy to write a book or give a lecture concerning the state of being happy and quite another thing to face the daily work-a-day world with its problems, stresses, frictions, jealousies and envy and feel this "happiness". However, if one begins to realize that one becomes unhappy because he emphasizes in his life the negatives of his surroundings and because he doesn't take the time to see the good around him in the present, then one realizes that he has created the unhappy state by his "emphasis in thought."

Why not simply learn to put the emphasis on a different place - on the positive - and take the time to look around for the good? Will this take any more time and effort than what one has been doing? Certainly not *and* it will bring about a happier condition within the individual and even make his "problem solving" task easier. There is nothing impractical about "looking for the good." The problems, stresses, hatreds, jealousies, etc. will not simply disappear but they will be much more easy to handle because of the individual's frame of mind. He will have the enthusiasm, the energy and the creative force to more adequately solve the problems! Unhappiness, depression, even from a material standpoint, have a most deterious effect on the individual; and he is not able to perform as effectively as he otherwise would. Hence, having a happy disposition, seeking a happy outlook, is quite practical in today's work-a-day world. There is nothing "PollyAnnish" about it - it is quite sound psychologically, medically and spiritually!

On his desk in Tokyo, the late General Douglas MacArthur kept a plaque concerning youth which could just as easily apply to happiness. It read: "Youth is not a time of life - it is a state of mind. You are as young as your faith, as old as your doubt; as young as your self-confidence, as old as your fear; as young as your hope, as old as your despair." Happiness and youth (youth in spirit) have just about everything in common!

Again, nothing I have said in this discourse should lead one to believe that as a Christian one does not have the right to be happy. *Happiness is a gift God gave man* but one that man himself must accept actively - must even work for. Happiness comes into our consciousness without our directly willing it - it comes into our awareness simply by our having worthwhile goals and by our ability to see the purity in what is around and within us. It is strictly an "inside job" of uncovering - revealing - to ourselves the great beauty of the Spirit that is within all. As Paul said, "God is in all, through all, with all." If we could just realize that "God is in all, with all and through all" the great joy, enthusiasm, *happiness* that would come to us!

The Eastern religions make much of the need to suffer to come into spiritual enlightenment. Jesus tells us that spiritual enlightenment comes to us through searching for the good which is in all, through all, with all. Maybe the two are not so far apart as at first it would appear. Don't most of us have to suffer greatly, have to feel that everything of this world has let us down, have to feel that our "backs are to the wall" before we make the effort to look within - to see the great beauty, help, understanding that is there? I believe most of us who profess Christianity *only give lip service* to the omnipresence of God *until* we

110

meet a situation in life when all temporal things have failed. Suddenly we are forced to look inward, and we find that there *is* an omnipresence of God. We are forced to suffer to learn God - we are forced to suffer to seek spiritual enlightenment. However, the great message of Jesus was that it is *not* necessary to suffer in order to have spiritual enlightenment - it is always there, ready for us, if we actively seek it. But most of us don't seek spiritual understanding and the happiness it brings until the world and "worldly things" have all failed us. The "happiness" that comes from spiritual enlightenment - not just the happiness, but the ecstasy as well - is always ready. What a great pity that for the most part the Christian world has failed to see the great message of Jesus to be that of saving us from the necessity of suffering - of giving us spiritual truths that, if followed, would bring us into the enlightenment without the suffering. Most of us, however, select the route of "suffering" before we open our minds and hearts to the message of salvation that was Jesus' great message. The word, salvation, itself explains how Jesus meant to free us from the necessity of suffering in order to have spiritual understanding - true happiness. Webster's defines "salvation" as "liberation from clinging to the phenomenal world of appearance and final union with ultimate reality." What could be more joyous, more happy, more wonderful then that - freedom from the phenomenal world of appearance and final union with ultimate reality! *The great message of Jesus was salvation - giving us a way to ultimate reality without suffering.* Because Western man refuses to open his eyes to the world of Jesus (to the Truth) he is forcing suffering upon himself. Hence, the Christian and the Eastern beliefs are not far apart in practice. But what a great loss to man in terms of his happiness and his understanding of his world, that he has not accepted the great gift of salvation!

If we are free of the shackles that worldly things and desire for worldly acclaim bring to us, we are truly able to see the greatness of nature, the greatness of others and ourselves - we are truly free. Then, if our ultimate goal in life is the raising of our spiritual consciousness (become more inner-aware) we have as our goal something that will make us happy no matter what adversities we have in life. We will be able to really live with enthusiasm, joyousness

111

and happiness in the Now because we *know* that we are growing in Christ Consciousness. The great message of Jesus was that he saved us from the necessity of suffering in order to find the way back home again - he made us free to be happy! What a shame that man has chosen not to receive this great gift until all else has failed - even when all worldly things have failed many cannot see this gift that is there for them because, as Paul tells us, they are too blinded by the god of this passing age to see the glory of the gospel.

We must recognize and remember that happiness is an inside job!

Real happiness is feeling a union with all energy, with all people, with all creation - it is love (both giving and receiving.) We have been given great lessons in how to enjoy life, how to realize the victorious and triumphant Spirit which is in us which is *real* happiness! All we have to do is practice the lessons we have been given - the light is there for us *Now*.

CHAPTER TWELVE

The Silence: The Abiding Place

After reading through the various chapters in this book, many will ask the questions, "Where must man's Spirit be when it is not being called upon - where is the home of Spirit?" and "is Spirit always at home ready to 'go out'?" The question that nearly all youngsters ask when discussing "Spirit" is "what do you mean by 'going within'?" To our world which is dominated by the senses - this extremely materialistic world - it seem inconceivable to many individuals that there is an "inner consciousness" of man - that there is an abiding place of Spirit which exists and is more real than anything which is visible in a material form. For such a large number of people nothing exists that cannot be detected by at least one of the senses. Yet, if these individuals would just look around them they would so quickly become aware of the many things that are known to exist because of their manifestations but are completely undetectable by any of our senses. Einstein in 1930 made the statement that our senses can detect only about one thousandth of what man knows exists in the electro-magnetic spectrum alone! And think of the discoveries since 1930! We all are aware of radio waves, television waves, x-rays, gravity, etc. that our senses do not detect - we recognize they exist because we see their manifestations. Certainly, if one will but open his eyes, ears, mind, and heart he will see thousands of manifestations of Spirit.

Isn't all creativity really a manifestation of Spirit, whether it be creativity in man or in nature? Any inventor, any artist, any effective manager, any composer, anyone

113

with a "new" idea had to "pull" that new "thing" or "idea" from somewhere - it always existed but it required that someone have faith, patience and a goal to make the new "manifest". That creative individual was manifesting the existence of Spirit and was drawing Spirit "out of its dormancy and from its secret place." It is literally true that "there is nothing new under the Sun." However, everything that we consider creative was "created" by someone who was *willing* to see "the visible in the invisible" - was able to recognize that much exists beyond what the senses detect and was not afraid to try to do something or "think" something that had not been done or thought before. The creative individuals of our world are drawing greatly on the victorious Spirit within them. They have not allowed the materialistic world to convince them that nothing exists except what the senses detect.

Have you ever stopped to think about how an invention came about, or how a new way of performing an "old job" was determined, or how a new composition was composed? Did not all the individuals who discovered the "new" simply take old concepts and look at them with new attitudes, with a sense of awareness that that was not all that could be? Have you ever examined the word, "discover"? Breaking it into its parts, one finds the roots of the word to be: "dis" and "cover". The "dis" means to "take away", to "remove". When one discovers anything he is revealing something that has always existed but has been covered over by an illusion that nothing existed "under the cover." Were not the Americas there before Columbus "discovered" them? Are not the things on the Moon there before we "discover" them? To discover simply means to "take the wraps off" so that our senses are now aware of what is there! However, if we rely on what our senses alone tell us nothing will be "unwrapped" or discovered.

The reason for my discussion of "discovery" and the limitation that sensory awareness alone placed upon us is to try to emphasize the fact that Spirit - the God-force - is always with us even though our sensory system may be unaware of that fact. Do not let the fact that your sensory system is limiting you make the only meaningful reality in life, the victorious Spirit within man, not exist for you! Take off the blinders that can be your sensory system and observe - discover or "unwrap" - the great Spirit that abides within your own world. *Discovering Spirit is the great discovery of man, but each man must discover Spirit for himself. It is the great secret of all time; but as with any secret, it only needs to be "discovered" to become a part of your everyday awareness and living.*

Where does one go to make the great discovery? Where lies the answer to the riddle of life? Where abides the victorious Spirit which is waiting to be discovered by each man for himself? What a marvelous thing - each man can become an explorer and heroic discoverer if only he be willing to search in the right place with the right motive. Each man must have a goal, faith and patience. The abiding place of Spirit is in the silence that exists within the human soul. To uncover the great victorious Spirit requires that man must look "within" and take the time to truly explore what is "within". No exploration, no discovery was ever made without having a goal, faith and patience.

Why has it been that down through the centuries men interested in spiritual enlightenment, men interested in creative ideas, men interested in true beauty, men interested in nature have all agreed concerning the greatness of silence? Is it simply that it is in the silence that beauty can be recalled? Partly, certainly, but so can misery, so can unhappy thoughts. So surely this is not the main or even an important reason.

The primary reason men have been so concerned and so interested in "silence" is that it is in the silence, whether it is consciously induced silencing of the mind or through sleep, that man comes into contact with his spiritual self - with his soul and the great beauty of his soul. It is in the silence and silence alone that man's creative aspects can come into activation. Certainly, these aspects of man may be manifest in consciousness and in outward manifestions but the contact is made in the silence. This is why so many of the great inventors, discoverers, artists, etc. have constantly stressed the need they have had for quiet contemplation and communion with nature. Charles Lindbergh, in a great letter in Life Magazine in July of 1969 made comments concerning the landing of man upon the Moon, and he stressed the need of man to get back to nature - to walk again in the wilds so that man could really bring technology into tune with the needs of man for spiritual understanding. Lindbergh, as have nearly all great

115

scientists and explorers, expressed the need for man to be close to nature and to "enter into silence" in order to really progress and grow. Whether we look at the works of a great philosopher such as Plato, a great scientist such as Einstein or Edison, a great playwright such as Shakespeare or Sophocles, or a great master teacher in the spiritual realm such as Jesus or Buddha, we find in all an emphasis on the importance of "going into the silence." All speak of the wonders of silence; all speak of the "wee small voice of conscience" that is found there; all speak of the great ideas that are found there; all speak of the great beauty that is there; all speak of man's need to tap this reserve of great energy, ideas, creativity and spiritual strength. Truly, in one way or another, through the ages most of the world's "great" men have spoken of the great power of the Spirit which is there ready to provide men with victory over all the temporal affairs of his world and ready to give man understanding of the true victory that is provided him when he truly contacts Spirit (God).

What is probably modern man's last almost completely undeveloped area of knowledge is an understanding of the importance of silence to man's physical, mental and spiritual well-being. Modern man has practically ignored this whole fertile field for scientific investigation. It has just been within the past few years that man has become even slightly aware of the importance of the silence and of meditation (prayer). In both *Science* and *Newsweek* during the month of March, 1970, there were reports of scientific "breakthroughs" in the understanding of what happens to individuals while in deep meditation (the silence.) Scientists have known for some time that the body is really a very complicated electro-magnetic system. There has been great evidence of the importance of concentration in activating the "power" within that system. It is in the silence (when the body and mind are at rest) that the "battery" of the human electro-magnetic system becomes charged - this has been demonstrated many times and much has been written concerning this fact by such outstanding scientists as Nicholas Tesla, Rudolf Steiner, Albert Einstein, Joshua Lederberg, etc. Actually, there are literally dozens of scientific "proofs" of the importance of going into "the silence" from a purely physiological and/or psychological standpoint.

However, the need to improve the physical condition of man is not the most important reason to enter the silence. The most important reason is that it is in the silence that one finds the abiding place of Spirit - it is here that one finds the "ingredients" that will allow him to utilize his victorious Spirit. It is in the silence that man can develop the third (spirit) side of man. As was stated earlier in this book, man is very much "three sided". Man must develop mind, body and spirit if he is to be truly balanced - if he is going to be able to "stand tall" and be at peace with himself and both the material and spiritual worlds. I like to think of man as a milking stool in terms of being balanced and having a proper foundation. A milking stool has three legs; and if one leg is missing or is much shorter than the other two, the stool will topple over or will be tipped and everything will slide off and be distorted. Man has understood a great deal about developing his mind through education, a great deal about developing and caring for his body; but he has been very neglectful in developing spirit. As a result man has not had a firm foundation - he has been unbalanced just as would be a milking stool if it had but two legs.

It is in the silence - through going "within" in prayer and meditation - that man develops his spirit side. It is in the silence that man comes into contact with his intuition, with the energizing force of Spirit.

Silence is fundamentally for the purpose of bringing man into an *understanding* relationship with victorious Spirit (God) - for developing the spiritual faculty, for communing with man's higher self.

Within all the important religions of the world, there is an emphasis on the importance of seeking the silence through meditation and prayer. In the Book of Matthew, Jesus tells us "Be still and know" and "When you pray, go into your room and shut the door and pray to your Father who is there in the secret place." Jesus, of course, is telling us that the "room" is the silence within; that we "shut the door" to keep out "worldly" "materialistic" things; that the "secret place" is the silence within; and we find the answer to the secret, the key, by seeking the silence through meditation and prayer and through recognizing that God is in all, through all, with all. In the Bible we are told, "What is seen was made out of things which do not appear." How

117

aptly this applies to the silence! Through the use of silence we may see some of "what does not appear". *But* what is most important is that we will come into a realization that Spirit is omni-present - it can be reached at any time and in any condition simply by going to the silence!

However, to seek "silence" without a strong goal, without faith in the existence of Spirit within the silence, is useless. One must have a goal - a reason with strong motivation - to make meaningful the search for the silence within. This is why I have touched on scientific verification of the physiological benefits of entering the silence, why I have mentioned the possible "seeing the visible in the invisible" there; *and,* most important to me, why I maintain that one can verify the "omni-presence and omni-potence of God" there. There must be a strong incentive - a strongly motivated goal - if one is to really embark on a program to discover the greatness, the beauty, the peace that exists within the silence.

No mind is capable of receiving instruction from any source when it is not dwelling on the goal. This has been clearly demonstrated in educational psychology and through many other areas of academic discipline. As Shakespeare said, "All the graces of mind and heart slip through the grasp of an infirm purpose." It is my certain knowledge, and the feeling of the great spiritual leaders of every major religion, that the fundamental reason (goal) for entering the silence is to establish a means of *conscious communication* between man and Spirit. Isn't this what is meant by Holy Communion - the communication between ourselves and God? It is through meditation and prayer in the silence that Holy Communion really takes place - not through ritual and not through special dogma. We should be going into the silence to find our true selves - the *true, real* man. The material body leaves us with this life; the worldly knowledge accumulated by the mind leaves us with this life; but Spirit (soul) never leaves us (no matter whether we believe in reincarnation or life after death in some other form) - and it is Spirit (our true, *eternal* self) which is to be found in the silence.

We are told that the "kingdom of God" is within - the spirit aspect of ourselves never dies. It is eternal! Shouldn't we commune with the one aspect of ourselves which is eternal, which has all knowledge of the true nature of God and the Universe and man?

If we had an aspect of our body that was not functioning correctly we would give and seek some type of attention to that problem. If we had an area of knowledge in which we were weak, we would try to bring enlightenment to it. Why do we ignore the Spirit? Why when we are depressed, when we are lonely, when we are unhappy won't we look "inside" in the silence and find the victorious Spirit that is our true selves there?

We have been given many great lessons in the fact that answers to so many of our problems - loneliness, unhappiness, despair, enslavement, etc. - can be found in the silence. In Isaiah 30:15, 16 it is stated, "Come back, keep peace, and you will be safe; in stillness and in staying quiet, there lies your strength." In Zachariah 2:13 it is written, "Be silent O all flesh before the Lord - he is raised up out of his holy habitation." In Romans 8:14 we are told, "For all who are moved by the Spirit of God are sons of God." In Philippians 4:5,6, Paul tells us, "The Lord is near; have no anxiety, but in everything make your requests known to God in prayer and petition with thanksgiving. Then the peace of God, which is beyond our utmost understanding, will keep guard over your hearts and your thoughts, in Christ Jesus." The literature of all the great religions give wonderful lessons concerning the peace, serenity, understanding, and love that comes to one by entering the silence through meditation and prayer.

It is in the silence that we really go beyond metaphysics and theology! We find and enter there the *true* consciousness - the Spirit aspect of ourselves which contains all knowledge, all power and all resources. I am not writing about worldly consciousness. Rather, I am writing about what Emerson would call the "oversoul" or Jung would call "collective consciousness". This is even higher than metaphysics because it is an individual thing - we do it alone and we are our own teacher, we are our own master. Metaphysics is very effective to use in groups but *true* consciousness (*cosmic* or *Christ* Consciousness) can *only* be discovered, used and known by the individual working alone in the silence!

It is Christ or Cosmic Consciousness - our victorious Spirit - that we should be seeking, where we return truly to our maker and all things become clear. The silence within is the true abiding place of Spirit even though it is our *real* abiding place too.

As in all things love plays the major role in developing our ability to go into the silence and find the victorious Spirit (cosmic consciousness) that is within us. We must recognize that God created each in his image. If we dislike ourselves, then we cannot find answers within ourselves. Likes attract and great consciousness will not be found within if we dwell in the silence on our limitations, on our weaknesses, on our material lacks. We must learn to love ourselves just as we must learn to love all other creatures of God.

We must recognize that God works through the power of love. The more loving we can become the closer to man's victorious Spirit we come. The closer to God we come through conscious love - of *all* things - the easier it is to enter into the silence and receive the abundant blessings and *all* wisdom that is there. We have been given great lessons in the importance of loving God. If we truly love God we love all things - others, ourselves, everything because God is in all, through all, with all!

There are 1440 minutes in a day - surely we can afford ten of those minutes (just 1/144) to tune into the higher forces of life - to all energy, to all power, to all wisdom. Think of the number of minutes each day we spend on body care and mind activity! For too long man has been developing only two sides of himself for almost all his waking hours - no wonder modern man is so shallow! He has not been giving himself any "depth" because he has been neglecting his third side (spirit) which is really the third dimension of man. Isn't it rather ridiculous to neglect the third side when it can be activated so easily? We really have an enormous amount of time in which to do this, and we should certainly be strongly motivated to do so!

Even after realizing the importance of going into the silence, many of us become terribly confused as to the various "techniques" we might use for entering the silence. Often we become so confused we abandon the whole idea. However, *the* technique for each man must be discovered by each individual for himself. There is a door; and if one knocks in sincerity, with faith, patience, and real motivation it will be opened. But each man must knock for himself - no one can knock for us. The key to open the door into the mysteries of the silence is given to each of us, but each must knock and insert the key. *There is no one method, no one way to enter the silence.* We are told in so many ways, in so many religions, *there are many roads to God* (man's victorious Spirit.) However, all the roads have silence in common - silent communion with non-worldly ideas and concepts. *The medium for communion is silent prayer and meditation.* How the medium is used, the technique that is utilized to silently pray and meditate, will vary with the individual; and he must not become "lost" in attempting to utilize the specific technique that someone else has found helpful. Lessons in praying and/or meditating can be helpful, but they can also be destructive because the road to victorious Spirit for one man may not be the road for another ("there are many roads to God.") Each man must knock for himself and each man will have to discover his own best road to God; but all do have in common a need to have a goal, faith and patience in regard to reaching the silence. Too often those who have become aware that the abiding place of man's victorious Spirit is in the silence have abandoned their attempts to enter the silence because they have become too preoccupied with techniques for "entering the silence." Motivation, faith and patience will open the door to the silence for any man; but no man can open the door to silence for another man!

It is true that the "pearl of great price" of which the Bible speaks is the silence. It is here that one really can release his victorious Spirit; it is here that one can really commune with God; it is here that the true secret and meaning for life can be found; it is here that man finds his peace, serenity, understanding, true wisdom and love. When one has truly entered the silence, worldly desires, preoccupations and problems are dissolved; and one truly knows that he has a great victorious Spirit which brings him real freedom, happiness, joy, love, company and enternal wisdom. When we truly enter the silence we communicate with our true selves and we enter the Kingdom of Heaven.

CONCLUSION

Man is coming into a new age in many respects. Certainly, there can be no doubt that this is the most technologically advanced and advancing period in the recorded history of mankind. It is also a period of time when life, because of man's great advancement in technological understanding, is becoming more and more impersonal. It is a time when many men feel caught up in a mass of de-humanizing machinery, technological language and impersonal contacts. Many have felt as though they were just a number - just a robot - carrying out what has been dictated to them by computers, electronic "monsters" and mass communicators. Most of us have become somewhat addicted to television and have learned to digest local, national and international news and events almost as soon as they occur. We have learned not to interpret news and events for ourselves but have willingly accepted whatever the "popular" newscaster and commentator has had to say. We have often become so addicted to the news media that we have not exercised our own intellect and our own powers of observation concerning events which may affect our lives. The commentator usually provides us with a rather simplistic evaluation of what is occurring. We become somewhat hypnotized into expecting that all events can be, and will be, interpreted by others for us. We have lost our own ability to observe and to really "see". We have abrogated our right and privilege to see the "visible in the invisible." It is no wonder that when we are faced with personal problems and personal relationships we flounder. We have not exercised our free will - we have allowed the mass media and the technology of our age to do our thinking for us. We do not have the time to look for the "good" as we are too interested in what the commentator has to say and we are hypnotized into believing what comes through the communication media. It should have been no surprise to man to discover that the Sixties were so senseless! We became so "blinded by the god of the passing age" (technology, television, material "things") that we ignored what is eternal - we turned almost completely from the victorious Spirit of man. We were isolated from the silence; we misunderstood the meaning of love; we distorted the "true" values in life; our churches became shrines to dogma, ritual and the passing whims of the times; we ignored the creative aspects of man; we subjected man to all types of psychological analysis forgetting that the great need of man is to have a sense of purpose and direction in his life; we allowed others to do our thinking for us and wondered why this "thinking" did not solve our problems; we allowed greed, jealousies, petty hatreds and avarice to govern us; we completely forgot that the spiritual nurturement of man is as essential to him as the material needs of the body and as knowledge to the mind.

Many of our young people adopted a new philosophy which completely renounced the "establishment" - an establishment which had forgotten its own roots and did not have a "sense of purpose". Many hailed the last decade as the beginning of the Aquarian Age (something very familiar to all students of metaphysics); but the Aquarian Age understood through metaphysics is a far different Age than the one envisioned by the typical youth. The metaphysician, who has been studying and evaluating the Aquarian Age for at least a half century and has stated it should start in the Sixties or early Seventies, has envisioned an age where man returns once again to his real purpose in life - the return to victorious Spirit. The metaphysican has written of the Aquarian Age as a period which would bring man into a fuller understanding of the importance of developing constructive attitudes, of a time when man would search for the good, of a time when material things would assume less importance than things of the Spirit, of a time when man would truly live in peace and harmony with all creatures. The Aquarian Age that we hear youth talking about is an age of license, an age of astrology, an age of witchcraft and an age of the occult. This youthful expectation of the Aquarian Age is merely another attempt by man to find a "crutch" - something he can blame for his weaknesses, his unhappiness, his alienation from our "technological" society, his evasion of personal responsibility. When we are depending on astrology, depending on "fortune tellers", we are again looking for "scapegoats" so that we can evade personal responsibility. When one says his astrological chart or his birth sign has said this or that will happen to him, isn't he saying that he has no free will? Isn't he denying that he has control over his action and attitudes? *Isn't he creating another "establishment" over himself which rules him just as effectively as the one he is revolting against?*

Man must stop being so "blinded by the god of this passing age" that he fails to realize that he has within himself the potential for the peace he so avidly seeks. We must stop looking to the material world for "crutches", for excuses and for blame. We must stop "passing the buck" for our personal failures and disappointments - whether we blame technology, the environment, the "establishment", astrological signs, or Ouija Boards. We must begin to realize that we create our world through our attitudes and that we can begin to live in a wonderful world - and become creative problem solvers - if we will only make an effort to understand our true nature. We must start realizing that we are as much in need of spiritual development as we are of physical and mental development. If we would start applying some of our great technology to more understanding of the effect of the thought process on our body and mind, we would begin to understand that we can have the type of age as the metaphysician envisioned the Aquarian Age. When man begins to realize the importance of the fact that the one thing in the world he can improve for certain is himself, he will quit his futile "spearing at windmills" and he will find that he can live in this technological, impersonal age with peace, harmony, joy, enthusiasm and can bring creative answers to what appear as insolvable problems.

In this little book I hope I have encouraged the reader to practice coming into tune with the infinite - with the great victorious Spirit of himself. Certainly, it is time that man ceased his search for "crutches", gave up his "blindness" due to the god of this passing age, stopped looking outside himself for both solutions and blame. The basic message that Jesus, and all the founders of all the lasting religions, has given man is a message of hope, salvation, understanding, peace, harmony and joy through looking at the infinite (victorious Spirit) with understanding. An understanding that man has a part of that infinite within himself and can always come into tune with it through prayer and meditation.

I am certain that some who pick up this book will feel "uncomfortable" in thinking about turning inward to find both peace and answers. I would hope that they will give it a try with an open mind and will recognize that their greatest obstacle to understanding any idea foreign to them is basically an attitude, and *attitudes can always be changed*. Has what you have been relying upon brought you peace, happiness and a greater awareness of the purpose of life? Have you a keen sense of direction for your life? If your answers are in any way negative, isn't the adopting of a new attitude a challenge to you? Don't you see a new opportunity in it? Tolstoy once said that stronger than all the armies of the world is an idea whose time has come. Perhaps the concepts examined in this book will bring into your life the strength of an idea whose time has come *for you*.

How much greater a world it could be if we truly all made an attempt to live by the Golden Rule; but perhaps we should interpret the Golden Rule as *"think* about others as you would have them *think* about you." Would not all attitudes then be of a positive nature? Would not the world then be looked at without glasses and with the crystal purity of Truth rather than through "the glass darkly?" If man is to ever live in harmony and happiness with the technological (material) aspects of his world, he will have to put into practice some of the lessons to which he has given only lip service for many centuries. Truly, with a change of attitude - with an attempt to find the real purpose in life which is to return to the victorious Spirit - this can be the dawn of the golden age of Aquarius. We have the tools to control the material world; we have the ability to harness much of nature; we have the knowledge to unlock the secrets of all the atoms of matter; and we have, but have not used, the information as to the means of releasing the great Spirit that is within us. If we put them *all* into action this will be man's finest hour; if we do not, it well could be the end of man.

Maybe we are on the threshold of a new and brighter age. Many people are looking for a spiritual foundation in their life and are seeking something of true and lasting value in their life. Once the message of the way in which man can release the victorious Spirit is truly understood, there will be no further need to keep searching without and grasping for crutches in the form of pseudo-sciences, the occult, astrology, etc. We can learn to harness the great technological advances of our time to create a truly better material world for all of us, but for that advancement to take place requires the releasing of the victorious Spirit within ourselves. The great, simple message of Jesus has for too long been "locked up" - kept secret - through dogma, ritual and attention to only temporal matters. By the application of intuitive knowledge, by understanding the wonders of nature, by applying intellect to find the "secret" in the message of all the great religions, by dropping the attempt to promote "personality" (the worldly self), by reaching into the silence for answers, man can bring this promise of a great age into being.

We should be heartened by the words found in Revelations 2:26, "To him who is victorious, to him who perserveres in doing my will to the end, I will give authority over the nations." In Revelations 3:12 it is said: "He who is victorious - I will make him a pillar in the temple of my God; he will never leave it."

In concluding this book, I hope that the reader will joyfully dwell on the words spoken by Paul in I Corinthians 2:9-15: "Things beyond our seeing, things beyond our hearing, things beyond our imagining, all prepared by God for those who love him, these it is that God has revealed to us through the Spirit. For the Spirit explores everything, even the depths of God's own nature. Among men, who knows what a man is but the man's own spirit within him? In the same way, only the Spirit of God knows what God is. This is the Spirit that we have received from God, and not the spirit of the world, so that we may know all that God of his own grace gives us; and, because we are interpreting spiritual truths to those who have the Spirit, we speak of these gifts of God in words found for us not by our human wisdom but by the Spirit. A man who is uninspired refuses what belongs to the Spirit of

God; it is folly to him; he cannot grasp it, because he needs to be judged in the light of the Spirit. A man gifted with the Spirit can judge the worth of everything."

ABOUT THE AUTHOR

Dr. Jack H. Holland has been a professor of Business Management for twenty-three years at San Jose State College in California. He has been a frequent lecturer in the Executive Development Program at Stanford Graduate School of Business. As a recognized expert in the field, he has conducted special courses for the National Association of Purchasing Management, the U. S. Chamber of Commerce, and various banking groups and associations. He was Chairman of the Management Department of San Jose State College from its inception in 1957 until 1968 when his lecture commitments around the world made it impractical for him to continue at that post.

Since that time he has continued as professor of Management and has been a frequent speaker to business and professional groups throughout the Western Hemisphere, and in the past two years, he has delivered more than 200 major addresses around the world. In spite of this, Jack Holland still finds time to serve as a member of the permanent consulting staff of three major corporations, and a frequent consultant to various other firms on problems of business management.

It may seem unusual to some that such an expert on the mundane problems of modern commerce should also be an ordained minister, scholar and lecturer on comparative religion, equally at home discussing Christianity, Judaism, Yoga, Islamic Law or Buddhistic cults. In reality, nothing could be more natural for this man who in the past five years, has been a lecturer at various churches almost every Sunday and has been particularly active with Unity churches, Churches of

Religious Science and Divine Science Churches. He has written frequently for various publications of the "New Thought" movement. He has been the leader for many Camp Farthest Out groups, many youth groups and for classes in self-motivation and self-understanding.

On his visit to the Orient in 1965, Jack Holland discovered for himself a key to the majestic serenity expressed so simply by the Dalai Lama and the other lamas at their refuge in Nepal. Dr. Holland, who had spent his life searching for answers for others, now found himself with an Answer which unites all of us in our quest for personal fulfillment. Thus the title of this book, "MAN'S VICTORIOUS SPIRIT".

P.74

If the missionaries had taught
Love and shared love ... the world
might be different today.